# Leadership in the Pharmaceutical Industry



*Leadership in the Pharmaceutical Industry* focuses on leadership in pharmaceutical organisations at three levels: individual, team, and organisational. At the individual level, it covers leadership basics, theories, types of leaders, differences between leaders and managers, leadership traits and skills, and systems thinking. At the team level, it explores leadership styles, the leader's interaction with the team, and employee motivation, including the use of intrinsic motivational factors. At the organisational level, it examines the leader's role in creating and maintaining organisational culture, forming and implementing organisational strategy, and managing organisational changes.

The book also addresses the specifics of the pharmaceutical industry, including the types and characteristics of innovations and the ethics of leader behaviour, emphasising the importance of ethical leadership. Notably, leadership issues are illustrated with practical cases featuring prominent leaders such as Paul Janssen, Daniel Vasella, Charles Walgreen III, John C. Martin, Roy Vagelos, Albert Bourla, Kiran Mazumdar-Shaw, and Filya Zhebrovska. These leaders were or are involved in creating, manufacturing, and providing patients with pharmaceutical products.

The book is designed to benefit readers from various business sectors, with the primary audience being academics, students, and individuals interested in leadership in the pharmaceutical industry.

**Nataliia Aliekperova** is a Lecturer in the School of Business Management & Creativity at Arden University, London, UK; Associate Professor in Organisation and Economics of Pharmacy Department at Bogomolets National Medical University, Kyiv, Ukraine.

## Routledge Focus on Business and Management

The fields of business and management have grown exponentially as areas of research and education. This growth presents challenges for readers trying to keep up with the latest important insights. *Routledge Focus on Business and Management* presents small books on big topics and how they intersect with the world of business research.

Individually, each title in the series provides coverage of a key academic topic, whilst collectively, the series forms a comprehensive collection across the business disciplines.

**Reimagining Organizational Change**
*Richard J. Badham and Brenda M. Santiago*

**Nostalgic Branding in the Toy Industry**
*Kamil Lubiński and Magdalena Grębosz-Krawczyk*

**Enterprise Evolution, Survival and the *Businesstype***
From Research to Practice
*Gianpaolo Abatecola*

**Grassroots Social Innovation**
The Role of Collaboration and Experiential Learning
*Karolina Osterczuk*

**Leadership in the Pharmaceutical Industry**
From Theory to Practice
*Nataliia Aliekperova*

For more information about this series, please visit: www.routledge.com/Routledge-Focus-on-Business-and-Management/book-series/FBM

# Leadership in the Pharmaceutical Industry

## From Theory to Practice

**Nataliia Aliekperova**

Routledge
Taylor & Francis Group
NEW YORK AND LONDON

First published 2025
by Routledge
605 Third Avenue, New York, NY 10158

and by Routledge
4 Park Square, Milton Park, Abingdon, Oxon, OX14 4RN

*Routledge is an imprint of the Taylor & Francis Group, an informa business*



ISBN: 978-1-041-01988-6 (hbk)
ISBN: 978-1-041-01990-9 (pbk)
ISBN: 978-1-003-61726-6 (ebk)

DOI: 10.4324/9781003617266

Typeset in Times New Roman
by KnowledgeWorks Global Ltd.

# Contents

# Abbreviations

| | |
|---|---|
| **AI** | Artificial Intelligence |
| **API** | Active Pharmaceutical Ingredient |
| **CDO** | Chief Digital Officer |
| **CEO** | Chief Executive Officer |
| **CCO** | Chief Operating Officer |
| **CX** | Customer Experience |
| **EDI** | Equity, Diversity and Inclusion |
| **ESG** | Environmental, Social, and Governance |
| **FDA** | Food and Drug Administration |
| **GMP** | Good Manufacturing Practice |
| **GxP** | Good 'x' Practice |
| **IQ** | Intellectual Quotient |
| **IT** | Information Technology |
| **ML** | Machine Learning |
| **MPD** | Mectizan Donation Program |
| **R&D** | Research & Development |
| **WBA** | Walgreens Boots Alliance, Inc |
| **WHO** | World Health Organization |

# Introduction

Leading companies in the pharmaceutical industry are organisations whose leaders strive to create innovative products that improve people's health and increase their well-being and quality of life. Even though leadership is a universal concept, each industry has its features, determined by the type of products, stakeholders, and infrastructure. Pharmaceutical companies are not just competitive; they are at the forefront of innovation, constantly pushing the boundaries of what's possible. Their leaders must make timely, balanced, and often non-standard decisions to keep up with the industry's pace. Professionalism and competence are essential components of pharmaceutical leadership. However, what sets leadership in the pharmaceutical industry apart is the critical importance of high moral and ethical principles, given the impact of pharmaceutical products on people's health and lives.

The book's purpose is a comprehensive study of leadership in organisations, using companies in the pharmaceutical industry as an example. The peculiarity of the book is not only the study of the theoretical foundations of leadership but also the detailed explanation of each of its aspects using actual practical examples. These examples from the pharmaceutical industry provide a clear understanding of how leadership theories and concepts are applied in real-world scenarios.

The book consists of eight chapters, each including the theoretical foundations of leadership and specific practical cases using the examples of leaders in the pharmaceutical industry such as Paul Janssen, Daniel Vasella, Charles R. Walgreen III, John C. Martin, Roy Vagelos, Kiran Mazumdar-Shaw, Filya Zhebrovskaya, and Albert Bourla. Their brief biographies are presented in the appendices.

The first chapter, 'Fundamentals of Leadership in the Pharmaceutical Industry', describes the main characteristics and evolution of leadership development, the concept of power in terms of leadership, and the similarities and differences between a leader and a manager.

The second chapter, titled 'Leadership Theories and Types of Leaders in the Pharmaceutical Industry', focuses on leadership theories, emphasising

DOI: 10.4324/9781003617266-1

transformational and adaptive leadership and different leader types, such as authentic leaders, inclusive leaders, level 5 leaders, and others.

Leadership implies the development of leadership traits and skills, such as systems thinking skills, as reflected in the third chapter of the book, 'Traits and Skills of Leaders in the Pharmaceutical Industry'.

As you know, a leader achieves business success not alone but together with their team. Therefore, it is vital to understand which leadership style of behaviour to choose in a given situation and how to build effective relationships with your team and develop them to achieve organisational goals. These are the issues considered in the book's fourth chapter – 'Leadership Styles and Team Leadership in the Pharmaceutical Industry'.

The fifth chapter of the book, 'Leadership and Motivation in the Pharmaceutical Industry', focuses on studying not only external factors of motivation but also internal ones, which contribute to the full involvement of employees in organisational issues.

The sixth chapter, 'Leadership Ethics and Innovations in the Pharmaceutical Industry', examines the features of leadership in the pharmaceutical industry, considering factors such as innovation compliance with ethical and moral standards. Specific examples of destructive leadership are also presented.

As is known, first, the leader creates an organisational culture, and then the organisational culture contributes to the formation of new leaders. The seventh chapter, 'Leadership and Organizational Culture in the Pharmaceutical Industry', examines issues devoted to studying the elements and levels of organisational culture, as well as the role of the leader in its formation.

To achieve sustainable development, the leader must be directly involved in forming the organisational strategy and implementing organisational changes. The eighth chapter, 'Leadership, Strategy and Organisational Changes in the Pharmaceutical Industry', will examine the main components of the organisation's strategy, as well as the types and stages of transformation implementation in the pharmaceutical industry.

The book is designed to benefit readers from various business sectors. The primary audience is academics, students, and individuals interested in leadership in the pharmaceutical industry.

# 1 Fundamentals of leadership in the pharmaceutical industry

## 1.1 Evolution, essence, and characteristics of leadership

The concept of leadership is of great interest to researchers, business people, politicians, and public figures. Burns (1978, p. 14) noted, 'Leadership is one of the most observed and least understood phenomena on earth'. Early in the last century, leadership was primarily seen as dominance, power, and the ability to influence people to earn their respect and admiration. However, in the 1930s, the trait approach emerged, highlighting the essential traits a leader should possess. Subsequently, in the 1940s, leadership began to be evaluated based on how effectively leaders behave in various situations. In the 1950s–1960s, leadership was viewed in the context of a common goal that unites leaders and their followers. In the 1970s and 1980s, there was a significant focus on studying the effective interaction between a leader and their followers, exploring how a leader can inspire them to achieve a shared objective. The 1990s further examined the leader's influence on followers, emphasising adapting people to changing conditions and challenges that require stepping out of their comfort zone (Northouse, 2021). Nowadays, a leader is considered an agent of change, a person who can effectively transform an ordinary organisation into a flagship of the world market. Leadership is becoming essential in forming a responsible and ethical worldview to develop various spheres of human activity, whether business or social.

The definition of leadership is not unambiguous and is primarily determined by the subjective vision of leadership theorists and practitioners. Thus, Rost (1991), studying the evolution of leadership development, identified about 200 definitions of leadership. Let us dwell on several definitions formulated by both researchers of leadership theory and famous personalities.

The 34th President of the United States, Dwight Eisenhower (1954), noted that a leader's influence is determined by achieving a specific goal. He stated that leadership is 'the art of getting someone else to do something that you want done because he wants to do it'.

DOI: 10.4324/9781003617266-2

British General Montgomery claimed, 'Leadership is the capacity and will to rally men and women to a common purpose and the character which inspires confidence' (Mercian, 2023).

Peter G. Northouse (2021, p. 6) noted, 'Leadership is a process whereby an individual influences a group of individuals to achieve a common goal'.

Gary Yukl (2006, p. 8) defines leadership as 'the process of influencing others to understand and agree about what needs to be done and how to do it, and the process of facilitating individual and collective efforts to accomplish shared objectives'.

Despite the numerous definitions of leadership, it is possible to identify several common characteristics that are inherent in this concept:

- ***Leadership comes from having followers.***
  Leaders do not act alone; they have followers who share their ideas and with whom they jointly achieve a common goal. Without effective teamwork, it is impossible to achieve the desired result. As the famous English proverb goes: 'No man is an island'.
- ***Leadership is driven by the ability to inspire people.***
  Leaders influence their followers by inspiring them, instilling confidence in their abilities, and providing opportunities to achieve a common goal. The leader's example, strength of character, and unyielding will to win are also crucial. As the wise Chinese proverb goes: 'Not the cry, but the flight of a wild duck leads the flock to fly and follow'.
- ***Leadership includes a shared purpose, which unites the leader and followers.***
  The existence of leadership is always conditioned by the presence of a common goal, which the leader inspires their followers to achieve. Former CEO of the pharmaceutical company Novartis Daniel Vasella stated: 'Your job is to recognise the right goal and path forward and then to align and persuade people to do the things you believe will be relevant for the long-term success of the company' (McKinsey & Company, 2012).
- ***Leadership is a process, not a single action.***
  Leadership is a process, not a single action, that involves the leader interacting with followers to achieve a desired outcome. As Warren Bennis noted, 'Leadership is the capacity to translate a vision into reality', but realising a leader's vision takes time and consistent action to achieve long-term goals (Weinfurter, 2013, p. 171).
- ***Leadership is determined not by formal powers but by personal qualities.***
  A person who occupies a high position in an organisation is not necessarily a leader if they cannot develop and transform the company, considering the influence of external factors. Peter Drucker noted: 'Effective leadership is defined by results, not attributes' (Upadhyay, 2019).
- ***Leadership is a transformation, including the deep values of people.***
  A leader inspires followers to achieve a common goal and can transform their values to achieve the desired result. A leader is an agent of change.

Burns (2003, p. 43) noted: 'Vigorous interaction between transforming leaders and their followers is itself a powerful causal force for change'.

- ***Leadership is achieving a humanistic result that contributes to further development.***
  Leadership should achieve a positive result that improves people's quality of life, such as creating pharmaceutical products to treat previously incurable diseases. Burns (2003, p. 16) drew attention to the human nature of leadership: 'Leaders working as partners with the dispossessed people of the world to secure life, liberty, and the pursuit of happiness'.

However, it is worth remembering that leadership is not always about setting great goals and striving for great ideas. Leadership can be unique and inherent in anyone ready to develop, take on additional responsibility, go the extra mile daily, grow professionally, and be effective. As Kouzes and Posner (2023) noted, leadership is not a privilege of a few charismatic men or women but a process by which ordinary people bring their best to others.

**Food for thought:** ***Identify leaders who embody leadership characteristics.***

**How it works in the pharmaceutical industry:** A description of leadership characteristics using the example of Janssen Pharmaceuticals founder, Paul Janssen (Lewi & Smith, 2007) (see Appendix A).

### Leadership comes from having followers

Paul Janssen's followers were the research team of professionals: chemists, pharmacologists, toxicologists, clinicians, statisticians, etc. Paul Janssen viewed his leadership role as an orchestra conductor, coordinating the work of various highly qualified specialists to achieve a common goal.

### Leadership is driven by the ability to inspire people

Paul Janssen inspired his followers by emphasising the importance of professional development, internal motivation, constant critical analysis, courage, and persistence in achieving goals and results. He noted, 'Many people are capable of doing much more than they believe'

(Gurowitz, 2015). Lab staff addressed him as Dr Paul, emphasising their respect and commitment.

**Leadership includes a shared purpose, which unites the leader and followers**

The shared purpose of Paul Janssen and his team was to create innovative drugs for treating various diseases, including pain relief, infections of multiple aetiologies, fungal diseases, psychiatry, gastroenterology, parasitology, cardiology, etc. In the laboratory of Paul Janssen, such well-known drugs as Haloperidol, Levamisole, Mebendazole, Miconazole, Loperamide, Fentanyl, Isopropamide Iodide, etc. were created.

**Leadership is a process, not a single action**

During the 40 years that Paul Janssen was Director of R&D at Janssen Pharmaceutica (Johnson & Johnson), 79 original drugs have entered the market. Eight medicines from Janssen are on the WHO List of Essential Medicines.

**Leadership is determined not by formal powers but by personal qualities**

Paul Janssen, the Director of R&D at Janssen Pharmaceutica, was a man of many personal and professional qualities. His sense of purpose, decisiveness, and self-discipline were evident in his work, as was his pursuit of new knowledge, intelligence, and creativity. He also had managerial talent, negotiation ability, and a unique vision for developing new drugs. His ability to visualise and design molecular structures when developing new chemical compounds was exceptional. Beyond his professional life, Paul Janssen was a man of diverse interests: he played the piano and chess, had a phenomenal memory, and was particularly fond of history.

**Leadership is a transformation, including the deep values of people**

Paul Janssen transformed the behaviour and values of his team through his leadership example. Maintaining high standards in developing new medicines became a transformational factor for the laboratory staff.

**Leadership is achieving a humanistic result that contributes to further development**

Paul Janssen's phrase can characterise the humanistic result of his work: 'There is so much more to be done; Patients are waiting' (Gurowitz, 2015). Paul Janssen's leadership approach has enabled the successful development of Janssen Pharmaceuticals, a Johnson & Johnson company division named a 2023 Fortune World's Most Admired Company and ranked #1 on the Pharmaceutical Industry list (Johnson & Johnson, 2023).

## 1.2 Types and features of leader's power

Leadership is closely linked to power, the ability to influence and impact an individual or a group. The renowned German sociologist, philosopher, and economist Max Weber (1968) defined power as the ability of an individual to achieve their goals despite the resistance of others. He identified three types of power: traditional, bureaucratic, and charismatic, each with unique characteristics and implications (Weber, 1968).

***Traditional authority*** is based on the belief in the inviolability of existing orders. In an organisation, it can be characterised as the presence of formal powers of the manager, according to the position they occupy. These formal powers are necessary to achieve organisational goals. For example, in the pharmaceutical industry, each organisation has its unique structure, all headed by managers endowed with formal powers. This type of power relates more to management than leadership, but it is the backbone of organisational success.

***Rational-legal authority*** is based on recognising legal norms and the validity of laws and regulations. It relies on complying with legislation, internal organisational regulations, procedures, and rules. The pharmaceutical industry is one of the most regulated industries in the world. For example, drugs must undergo state registration; the quality system of medicines from the moment of their creation to delivery to the patient is ensured by compliance with Good 'x' Practice (GxP) standards, the production or distribution of pharmaceutical products requires a licence, etc. The power of leaders in the pharmaceutical industry is not just about understanding the specifics of industry regulation but also about their ability to interact with stakeholders, influencing the industry's direction effectively.

***Charismatic authority*** is based on the exceptional trust of followers in the leader's personalities and ideas. This type of power is the most associated with leadership, as it is based on the leader's personal characteristics. All outstanding leaders in the pharmaceutical industry had personal charisma, reflected in their commitment to the vision of the organisation's development, passion for achieving goals, and ability to inspire people in times of difficulty and uncertainty.

Some of the most used types of power in the science of leadership and management were those formulated by French and Raven (1959): coercive, reward, legitimate, referent, and expert.

***Coercive authority***, rooted in the fear of punishment for failure to complete assigned tasks, such as fines, deprivation of bonuses, and demotions, is a power that, despite its simplicity, should be avoided. It demotivates employees and deteriorates their work quality, proving ineffective in achieving long-term goals.

***Reward authority*** is based on providing material and non-material incentives for effectively implementing assigned tasks. Its disadvantage is the limited financial resources for paying bonuses, increasing wages, the possibility of promotion, etc.

***Legitimate authority*** is based on the belief that the leader has the necessary authority to make decisions and manage people. In an organisation, this is generally determined by the presence of functional responsibilities that correspond to a particular position.

***Referent authority*** is based on the leader's personality and their ability to interact with people effectively. A positive example of a leader with referent power inspires employees to enhance their professionalism and motivates them to pursue self-improvement and development.

***Expert authority*** is similar to referent authority; however, it is based to a greater extent on the leader's high level of competence and professionalism, which causes respect among followers and trust in his ideas.

The ***referent*** and ***expert*** types of power reflect the charismatic power proposed by Weber and relate to ***personal power***, which allows the leader to inspire followers and promote their active involvement in achieving the organisation's vision.

**Food for thought: *Which type of power is more important?***

**How it works in the pharmaceutical industry:** A description of personal power is given using the example of the former CEO of the biopharmaceutical company Gilead Science, John C. Martin (see Appendix B).

## Referent authority

- John C. Martin, despite his modesty, was a visionary who, in 20 years, transformed Gilead Science into a global biopharmaceutical company with a market capitalisation of $120 billion (Lou et al., 2022).

- John C. Martin possessed personal qualities that allowed him to be identified as a leader (responsibility, purposefulness, focus on results, innovativeness, passion, etc.).
- Dr Martin mentored his team members, inspiring them to develop their start-ups and business ideas, for example, setting up Kronos, headed by the former head of R&D at Gilead Science (Wright, 2021).
- Dr Martin was an example for his employees as a successful and enterprising leader, a brilliant scientist, and a person who constantly strived for high standards in creating innovative antiviral drugs. He noted, 'We must continue to innovate to make our own products obsolete' (Lou et al., 2022).

### Expert authority

- John C. Martin was an expert in biopharmaceuticals: he received a BS in chemical engineering, then a PhD in organic chemistry from the University of Chicago. He worked as a researcher, research team leader, director of antiviral chemistry, and head of R&D. From 1996 to 2016, he served as CEO of Gilead Science (Lou et al., 2022).
- Dr Martin also received an MBA in marketing, which allowed him to make Gilead Science a successful patient-centric company and establish collaboration with top researchers, clinicians, the patient community, etc. (Lou et al., 2022).
- As a scientist, Dr Martin contributed to 34 patents and 85 publications (Li & De Clercq, 2022). He also inspired his team to integrate scientific theoretical knowledge with practical experience to create breakthrough innovative drugs.
- Dr Martin received wide public recognition for his scientific activities and global contribution to the creation of antiviral drugs that have saved the lives of millions of people. Harvard Business Review ranked John C. Martin as one of the 'Best Performing CEOs in the World' (Garabedian, 2021).

## 1.3 Similarities and differences between leader and manager

While studying leadership, it's important to understand the distinct roles of leaders and managers. As the key administrator in an organisation, managers are entrusted with managing people and processes. Their functions include planning, organising, motivating, and monitoring the performance of employees in their assigned tasks. As Drucker (2001, p. 10) noted: 'Management is about human beings. Its task is to make people capable of joint performance, to make their strengths effective and their weaknesses irrelevant'.

The number of managers, their area of responsibility, and job titles depend on the specifics of the organisation's activities, its size, and other factors. The importance of an effective manager in an organisation is difficult to overestimate. Their daily monitoring of task completion is not just a routine but a necessity, without which the leader's vision and strategy cannot be realised. Stanford University professor Robert Sutton (2010) noted, 'When we glorify leadership too much, and management too little, there is great risk of failing to act on this obvious but powerful message'.

Management and leadership share similar functions, such as working with people, achieving goals, and utilising power. However, there are also significant differences. As a norm, a leader envisions the company's development and executes its transformation. In contrast, a manager focuses more on maintaining the status quo by organising functional processes within an established system. What sets a leader apart from a manager are their personal qualities, which reflect their worldview and empower them to influence people effectively and inspire them to achieve goals. As Bennis and Goldsmith (2010) stated, managers do things right, and leaders do the right thing.

Former CEO of global pharmaceutical company Novartis, Daniel Vasella, noted that a company director must have both managerial and leadership skills. He attributed management to the ability to create systems and processes, organisational strategy, and the ability to organise and plan. Leadership, according to Vasella, is the ability to make a compelling purpose, articulate clear values, inspire and engage people, and manage change. Leadership competencies are more challenging to develop and learn since they primarily involve character, internal motivation, interpersonal skills, etc. Daniel Vasella emphasised that 'leadership development must involve introspection, reflection, and examination of our patterns' (Cashman, 2013).

According to Kotter (1990), the functions of a leader and a manager can be differentiated as follows:

1 ***A leader establishes direction*** (forms a vision for the organisation's development, creates a 'picture of the future', and defines strategy and critical goals), while ***a manager plans and budgets*** (agrees with the leader on goals and targets and allocates resources within a specific time frame).
2 ***A leader aligns people*** (creates a team, discusses and adjusts goals with managers, and builds commitment to their ideas), while ***a manager organises and staffs*** (establishes procedures and rules, selects and places personnel, distributes tasks, and ensures the process of completing assigned tasks).
3 ***A leader motivates and inspires*** (inspires employees to achieve goals; stimulates internal motivation, the desire for development and self-improvement), while ***a manager controls and solves problems*** (develops

incentives and motivation for employees, promotes the generation of creative ideas, monitors the implementation of tasks, and eliminates issues).

**Food for thought:** ***What consequences might the organisation face if the leader assumes the functions of a manager?***

**How it works in the pharmaceutical industry:** The functional differences between the US drugstore chain Walgreens leader Charles R. Walgreen III and managers under Kotter's theory (1990) (Collins, 2001) (see Appendix C).

### A leader establishes direction

- Charles Walgreen focused only on the development of the pharmacy chain.
- Charles Walgreen envisioned the company's growth as the most convenient pharmacy, maximising profitability per customer visit.
- The strategies for developing the Walgreens pharmacy chain were based on established theories: cost leadership, differentiation from M. Porter, and market development from I. Ansoff.

### A manager plans and budgets

- Managers, due to strategic reasons, had to sell the rest of the Walgreens business (about 500 restaurants, etc.) within four years.
- Managers had to open new pharmacies at street corners to increase the number of customers and improve customer service.
- The strategy was designed with clear goals, such as increasing the availability of pharmaceutical care and the company's profitability through economies of scale and by increasing the average check.

### A leader aligns people

- Charles Walgreen consistently followed the planned development of the pharmacy chain to increase its profitability, effectively involving his team in this process.
- As the company evolved, new goals were set and discussed with the team. Charles Walgreen was the protagonist of innovation and helped to proliferate an innovative approach in his team.

**A manager organises and staffs**

- According to the plan, managers had to sell assets and expand the pharmacy network promptly. A programme for effective pharmacy management was also introduced, and a new approach was used – calculating profitability per client.
- In the early 1980s, the management team implemented the Intercom electronic network, making Walgreens a 'neighbourhood drugstore' for every customer, introducing a computerised inventory control system, etc.

**A leader motivates and inspires**

- Charles Walgreen assembled a solid, motivated management team that effectively implemented all innovations.
- Charles Walgreen trusted his managers, recognised and was proud of their successes and achievements, and was distinguished by his modesty.
- Charles Walgreen has trained successful successors to develop Walgreens further.

**A manager controls and solves problems**

- Operational managers had full authority to implement assigned management tasks.
- After making decisions, managers motivate and monitor employees' work by their area of responsibility.
- After the departure of Charles Walgreen, the company continued to thrive, using the professionalism and motivation of the management team.

## 1.4 Conclusions

1 Leadership, as a science, is a constantly evolving field. Initially, a leader was often seen as someone who wielded dominance. However, with the advent of leadership theories, the focus has shifted to personal traits, behaviour in various situations, interaction with followers, and the organisation's transformation. Leadership is a blend of characteristics that reflect its essence: the ability to inspire followers, the presence of a common goal, authenticity, and the transformation process to achieve a humane result.

2 The capability to exert power and influence is essential in leadership. Leadership, which leads to exceptional and long-lasting outcomes, relies on both formal (positional) and personal power. Personal power, which reflects leadership competencies, is a crucial factor in this equation. It can be seen as a referent and an expert authority. Referent authority is rooted

in the leader's personality and ability to engage with people effectively. Expert authority stems from the leader's high expertise, which fosters trust in the leader and their ideas.

3 Leadership and management share similar characteristics, such as goal achievement, power, authority, and working with people. However, they are distinct concepts. A leader transforms a system based on their vision and personal traits, such as the ability to inspire people. On the other hand, a manager is more focused on regulating and improving processes within an existing system.

## References


Bennis, W., & Goldsmith, J., (2010). *Learning to Lead: A Workbook on Becoming a Leader*. 4th edition. New York: EasyRead Large.

Burns, J.M., (1978). *Leadership*. New York: Harper & Row.

Burns, J.M., (2003). *Transforming Leadership: A New Pursuit of Happiness*. New York: Atlantic Monthly Press.

Cashman, K., (2013). A global leader's perspective on CEO leadership: Part one. *Forbes*, 5 June 2013. Available from: https://www.forbes.com/sites/kevincashman/2013/04/18/a-global-leaders-perspective-on-ceo-leadership-part-one-2/ [Accessed 19 December 2023].

Collins, J., (2001). *Good to Great*. London: Random House Business Books.

Drucker, P., (2001). *Essential Drucker*. London: Routledge.

Eisenhower, D.D., (1954). Remarks at the Annual Conference of the Society for Personnel Administration. *The American Presidency Project*, 12 May 1954. Available from: https://www.presidency.ucsb.edu/node/231971 [Accessed 23 November 2023].

French, J.R.P. Jr., & Raven, B., (1959). The bases of social power. *Studies in Social Power*. pp. 150–167.

Garabedian, C., (2021). The glory of John Martin: An understated leader who built a biotech powerhouse. Timmerman Report, 5 April 2021. Available from: https://timmermanreport.com/2021/04/the-glory-of-john-martin-an-understated-leader-who-built-a-biotech-powerhouse/ [Accessed 15 December 2023].

Gurowitz, M., (2015). The legacy of Dr. Paul Janssen: How a "funny idea" helped change the course of modern medicine. *Johnson & Johnson*, 11 September 2015. Available from: https://www.jnj.com/the-legacy-of-dr-paul-janssen-how-a-funny-idea-helped-change-the-course-of-modern-medicine [Accessed 11 December 2023].

Johnson & Johnson, (2023). *Johnson & Johnson Named a 2023 Fortune World's Most Admired Company and Ranked #1 on the Pharmaceutical Industry List*. Johnson & Johnson Services, Inc. Available from: https://www.jnj.com/latest-news/johnson-johnson-named-a-2023-fortune-worlds-most-admired-company#:~:text=For%20the%2021st%20year,for%20the%20tenth%20consecutive%20year [Accessed 10 December 2023].

Kotter, J.P., (1990). *Force for Change: How Leadership Differs from Management*. New York: The Free Press.

Kouzes, J.M., & Posner, B.Z., (2023). *The Leadership Challenge: How to Make Extraordinary Things Happen in Organisations*. 7th edition. Hoboken, NJ: John Wiley & Sons, Inc.

Lewi, P.J., & Smith, A., (2007). Successful pharmaceutical discovery: Paul Janssen's concept of drug research. *R&D Management*, 37(4), 355–362. https://doi.org/10.1111/j.1467-9310.2007.00481.x

Li, G., & De Clercq, E., (2022). A medicinal chemist who reshaped the antiviral drug industry: John Charles Martin (1951–2021). *Medicinal Research Reviews*, 42(2), 647–653. https://doi.org/10.1002/med.21858

Lou, L.L., Flood, A., Yang, T., & Whitley, R.J., (2022). Commentary: John C. Martin (1951–2021). *Antiviral Therapy*, 27(2). https://journals.sagepub.com/doi/full/10.1177/13596535211067895

McKinsey & Company, (2012). Leading in the 21st century: An interview with Daniel Vasella. McKinsey & Company. Available from: https://www.mckinsey.com/~/media/McKinsey/Featured%20Insights/Leading%20in%20the%2021st%20Century/An%20interview%20with%20Daniel%20Vasella/Daniel_Vasella.pdf [Accessed 4 December 2023].

Mercian, T.O., (2023). Harnessing network leadership in the British Army. *Leadership Insight*, 44. Available from: https://www.army.mod.uk/media/23774/cal-leadership-insight-no44-network-leadership.pdf [Accessed 25 November 2023].

Northouse, P.G., (2021). *Leadership: Theory and Practice*. 9th edition. Los Angeles, CA: Sage Publications.

Rost, J.C., (1991). *Leadership for the Twenty-First Century*. New York: Praeger.

Sutton, R.I., (2010). True leaders are also managers. *Harvard Business Review*, 11 August 2010. Available from: https://hbr.org/2010/08/true-leaders-are-also-managers [Accessed 17 December 2023].

Upadhyay, S., (2019). Results and empathy. *Medium*. Available from: https://upadhyay-sanjay.medium.com/results-and-empathy-2702f97ce0c [Accessed 11 December 2023].

Weber, M., (1968). *Economy and Society: An Outline of Interpretative Sociology* (Vol. 1). New York: Bedminster Press.

Weinfurter, D.J., (2013). *The Keys to Effective Leadership*. New York: Palgrave Macmillan.

Wright, R., (2021). John C. Martin, a much-missed mentor and Kronos Bio board member. *Life Science Leader*, 23 August 2021. Available from: https://www.lifescienceleader.com/doc/john-c-martin-a-much-missed-mentor-and-kronos-bio-board-member-0001 [Accessed 15 December 2023].

Yukl, G., (2006). *Leadership in Organisations*. 6th edition. New York: Pearson-Prentice Hall.

# 2 Leadership theories and types of leaders in the pharmaceutical industry

## 2.1 Classification and brief characteristics of leadership theories

Although leadership has been an object of study for a long time, new studies have been initiated, the results of which are reflected in leadership theories. At present, the central leadership theories can be classified into the following clusters:

- Leadership theories focused on ***the personality of the leader***.
- Leadership theories focused on ***followers and the structure of tasks***.
- Leadership theories focused on ***the relationship between the leader and followers*** (see Figure 2.1).

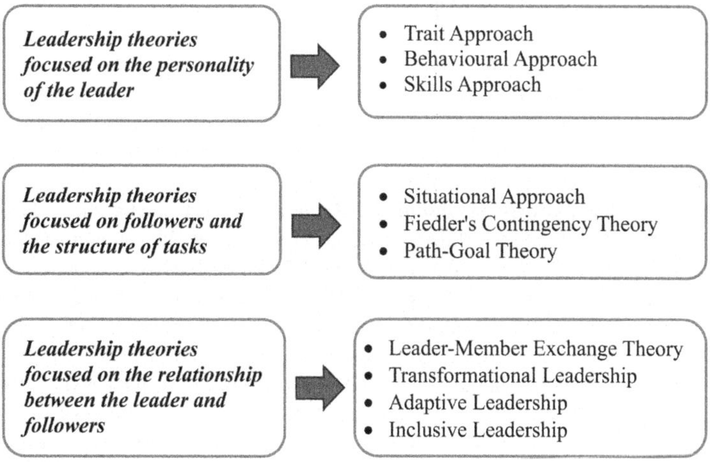


*Figure 2.1* Classification of leadership theories.

DOI: 10.4324/9781003617266-3

In leadership theories that focus on ***the personality of the leader***, the main emphasis is on studying the characteristics of the leader's personality. In 1948, Ralph Stogdill, based on a literature review, identified the most optimal traits that make an ordinary person a leader. The trait approach was created based on the knowledge obtained. Later, in 1974, Stogdill revised and changed the leadership traits list. In addition, other researchers proposed sets of leadership traits (Aliekperova & Aliekperov, 2023) (see Section 3.1).

***Behavioural theories*** propose that leaders exhibit two main types of behaviour: task and relationship orientation. The first studies on behaviour theories were conducted in the 1950s at Ohio University (Hemphill & Coons, 1957) and the University of Michigan under the guidance of Likert (Likert, 1961, 1967). In the 1960s, Robert Blake and Jane Mouton furthered this research by formulating five models of leader behaviour in an organisation, based on task or relationship orientation, in their managerial (leadership) grid theory (Blake & Mouton, 1985). Today, researchers continue to explore the behavioural approach to leadership, particularly in the context of the dynamic changes in the organisational environment (Behrendt et al., 2017).

***The skills approach*** focuses on the competencies that a leader must possess. Robert Katz (1955) proposed a model of three leadership skills – technical, human, and conceptual – at three management levels: low, middle, and top management. Later, Mumford et al. (2000) formulated a skill-based model of leadership, which consists of five components: competencies, individual attributes, career experiences, environmental influences, and leadership outcomes (performance and problem-solving) (see Section 3.2).

In ***follower-oriented and task-structured leadership theories***, the effectiveness of leader behaviour in an organisation is viewed in terms of the influence of various situational factors.

According to ***the situational approach by Hersey and Blanchard***, a leader chooses their behaviour style depending on employees' level of professional and motivational maturity (see Section 4.1). The authors identify the following leadership styles: directing, coaching, supporting, and delegating (Hersey & Blanchard, 1996; Blanchard et al., 2013).

According to ***Fiedler's contingency leadership theory***, the leader's behaviour style (task or relationship) is contingent on understanding situational factors (Fiedler, 1967). These factors, such as the relationship between the leader and subordinates, the structure of the task, and the leader's authority, play a crucial role in effective leadership. For example, if the relationship between the leader and employees is good, the task is structured, and the authority is strong, the leader should focus on the task. However, if, for instance, the relationship between the leader and employees is good, but the task is unstructured, and the leader's authority is weak, then people orientation would be appropriate.

***The path-goal theory***, developed by House and Mitchell (1974), is a powerful tool for leaders to motivate and support their employees in achieving goals. Depending on the followers and task characteristics, the leader can choose from four behaviour styles (directive, supportive, participative, and achievement-oriented). The achievement-oriented leadership style, in particular, is highly effective when tasks are clear and well-structured, the group is cohesive and goal-oriented, and there's a high level of self-assessment of professional competencies.

It is worth noting that leadership theories focused on followers and task structure are prescriptive and provide specific recommendations on how a leader should behave in a given situation.

Theories focusing on ***the relationship between leader and followers*** emphasise the importance of developing, supporting, and inspiring employees to achieve organisational goals effectively.

Graen and his colleagues developed ***the leader-member exchange theory (LMX Theory)*** in the 1970s (Graen & Cashman, 1975; Dansereau et al., 1975). According to LMX Theory, the relationship between a leader and followers is formed according to the principle: in-group or out-group. A high level of mutual trust and respect characterises in-group relationships. Employees are involved in the decision-making process, and effective communications are established between them and the leader. As a result, the company develops more successfully in the short- and long-term. Formal relationships between the leader and employees characterise out-group relationships. The leader's task is to transform relationships with employees from out-group to in-group.

The essence of ***the transformational theory*** is the ability of a leader to implement transformations in an organisation and achieve performance beyond expectations through developing followers, paying attention to their needs, inspiring them, etc. (Bass, 1985, 1990) (see Section 2.2).

Heifetz and colleagues in the 1990s formulated ***the adaptive theory*** of leadership (Heifetz, 1994; Heifetz et al., 2009). An adaptive leader helps to mobilise, motivate, orient, and focus people on challenges and changes that often require going outside their 'comfort zone'. The adaptive leadership model consists of three sequential, interrelated components:

- Situational challenges
- Leader behaviours
- Adaptive work

Situational challenges are divided into technical and adaptive. The leader can address technical challenges, and the solution is usually based on existing experience and habitual behaviour. Adaptive challenges are of most interest, as they require followers' involvement, often changing their behaviour patterns, values, way of thinking, etc.

Leader behaviours involve supporting and coordinating followers in the process of changing their behaviour through the following steps:

1 Get on the Balcony
2 Identify the Adaptive Challenge
3 Regulate Distress
4 Maintain Disciplined Attention
5 Give the Work Back to the People
6 Protect Leadership Voices from Below

Adaptive work is creating a holding environment that promotes compelling motivation and orientation of people to solve adaptive problems, as well as productive interactions between the leader and followers.

New leadership theories, such as ***inclusive leadership***, are currently emerging and have arisen in response to new challenges in a multicultural global environment. This theory highlights the importance of creating an inclusive approach, which leads to positive organisational outcomes (Northouse, 2021).

> **Food for thought: *Identify the most important challenges for adaptive leaders.***

**How it works in the pharmaceutical industry:** Description of adaptive leader behaviours using the interaction between Pfizer CEO Albert Bourla and his employees during the COVID-19 pandemic (National Journal, n.d.) (Appendix D).

> **Get on the balcony**
>
> When Albert Bourla took the reins as CEO of Pfizer in January 2019, he had already initiated a transformation to make the company more adaptive, digital, and capable of solving complex problems. This strategic shift allowed the new leader to envision the potential for creating an antiviral vaccine in record time – 6–9 months, a significant departure from the industry's traditional 8–10 years. Bourla's leadership was marked by his principle of having the courage to think big (Gulland, 2020).

## Identify the adaptive challenge

*Technical challenges* include providing the COVID-19 vaccine development process with the necessary resources, forming a SWAT team of 11 leading Pfizer employees, creating the Global COVID-19 Medical Service Program to engage healthcare professionals in the fight against coronavirus, and forming crucial partnerships with other stakeholders.

*Adaptive challenges* include finding and selecting the optimal vaccine development technology promptly and effectively resolving issues related to vaccine development across the entire value chain (R&D, manufacturing, logistics, transportation, etc.).

## Regulate distress

Creating a new antiviral vaccine using the still poorly understood mRNA technology in the shortest possible time was a global challenge for Pfizer and was associated with high risk. To make this possible, Albert Bourla, the company leader, not only demonstrated courage and persistence but also inspired his team and employees. Dr Bourla paid great attention to the proliferation of organisational values. For example, the slogan 'Science will win' became one of the corporate symbols of employees' involvement and motivation in creating a vaccine.

## Maintain disciplined attention

Such a global challenge as creating a vaccine in a few months was associated with many difficulties and challenges at every stage of the value chain, for example, organising the production of three billion doses and observing the conditions for transporting a heat-labile vaccine worldwide. Albert Bourla relentlessly demanded that his employees find solutions to problems despite their doubts about the project's success. As he later noted, people always find the best solution to problems if they persistently do not retreat from the goal.

## Give the work back to the people

Albert Bourla was confident in the professionalism and motivation of Pfizer employees, delegating their decision-making on critical issues related to the creation of a vaccine against COVID-19. For example, his SWAT team members proposed and scientifically substantiated the feasibility of mRNA technology in creating an antiviral vaccine.

Despite the risks, Albert Bourla decided to follow his team's recommendation. This decision led to a successful and productive cooperation with the German biopharmaceutical company BioNTech SE.

**Protect leadership voices from below**

Albert Bourla's leadership was pivotal in restructuring Pfizer into a global company that could adapt rapidly and effectively in the face of uncertainty. To form a competitive edge, he committed to providing resources and support to those employees who could deliver effective solutions to elevate healthcare standards and improve patients' health and quality of life worldwide.

## 2.2 Transformational and transactional leadership

The essence of transformational leadership theory is the practical ability of a leader to transform an organisation to achieve goals through mutually beneficial interactions with followers. Burns (1978) noted in his early research in the late 1970s that this practicality is crucial for forming bonds between leaders and followers that enhance mutual motivation and morality. Burns (2003, p. 44) emphasised that 'instead of exercising power over people, transforming leaders champion and inspire followers'.

In the 1980s, Bass (1985) supplemented and expanded Burns's transformational theory, primarily focusing on its use in business. The following features of transformational leadership were identified: idealised influence, inspiring motivation, intellectual stimulation, and individualised consideration.

- ***Idealised influence*** is the formulation by the leader of a clear vision of the organisation's development, understandable and essential values for employees, and ethical standards. This creates an atmosphere of mutual trust and readiness for organisational changes.
- ***Inspiring motivation*** is inspiring people to achieve their goals, encouraging them confidently and enthusiastically, and explaining the importance and necessity of implementing planned initiatives.
- ***Intellectual stimulation*** not only promotes the development of followers' intellectual potential but also empowers them, supporting individual initiatives and fostering openness to new ideas.
- ***Individualised consideration*** is about more than just training and developing people. It's about valuing their unique values, abilities, and aspirations to identify and develop their strengths, fostering personal growth and a sense of importance.

Despite the importance of transformational leadership factors, they usually go hand in hand with transactional ones. Bass (1990) considered transactional leadership as a necessary element in business leadership, which does not provide for a superior leadership position but only a mutually beneficial exchange between the leader and followers. Bass and Avolio (1994) highlighted the following transactional leadership factors:

- ***Contingent reward*** – an exchange between a leader and followers in which the effect of the subordinates' activities is exchanged for providing them with a particular reward. Contingent reward is an effective tool for achieving organisational goals, as it involves setting clear and understandable goals and the expected reward for achieving them.
- ***Management-by-exception (MBE) active*** – monitoring employee errors while performing tasks and adjusting their actions to achieve the desired result. MBE – active leadership does not have a noticeable impact on employee performance.
- ***Management-by-exception (MBE) passive*** – no intervention in performing tasks, responding only to the consequences of errors and problems that have arisen. MBE – passive leadership is an ineffective management tool.

A factor such as ***laissez-faire leadership*** was also identified, which implies a lack of leadership when the leader avoids responsibility, postpones decision-making, does not provide feedback to employees, etc. Avolio (1999, p. 55) noted that laissez-faire leadership is 'poor, ineffective leadership and highly dissatisfying for followers'.

Transactional factors are essential for the business environment, but they are not enough for the effective and long-term development of the organisation. When combined with transactional factors, transformational leadership enhances the effect and allows for 'performance beyond expectation' (Bass & Avolio, 1994). Bass (1998, p. 5) stated, 'Transformational leadership styles build on the transactional base in contributing to the extra effort and performance of followers' (see Figure 2.2).

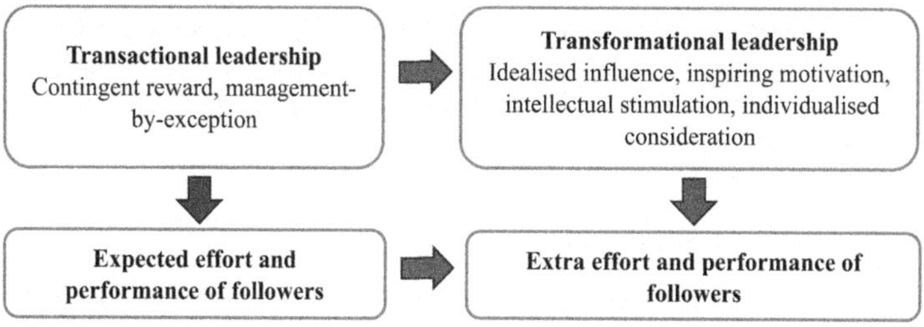


*Figure 2.2* The interconnection between transformational and transactional leadership.

**Food for thought:** ***What traits and skills are needed to be a transformational leader?***

**How it works in the pharmaceutical industry:** Description of the factors of transformational leadership using the example of the founder of Janssen Pharmaceuticals, Paul Janssen (Lewi & Smith, 2007) (Appendix A).

### Idealised influence

Paul Janssen viewed the laboratory as a profit centre due to the creation of new patentable inventions. He set high productivity expectations, often reminding his team, 'The patients are waiting' (Gurowitz, 2015). However, he also played a crucial role in fostering an internal atmosphere of mutual trust and respect. This unique balance allowed the laboratory to function more like a living organism, with new inventions and discoveries often being unplanned and unpredictable. Dr Paul valued his employees' high professionalism, courage, persistence, and curiosity.

### Inspiring motivation

Paul Janssen was sure the laboratory should employ self-motivated people who strive for a specific result – creating new effective drugs. He noted: 'Many people are capable of doing much more than they believe' (Gurowitz, 2015). At the same time, Paul Janssen understood that the research process was associated with difficulties and delays, so he supported, encouraged, and inspired his employees and recognised their achievements. Paul Janssen stimulated the research process with his famous question, 'What's new?' when he made his daily rounds of the laboratory. He also synchronised the work of various specialists and departments, which was reflected, for example, in the publication of research results in academic journals. This also had a motivating effect on the employees.

### Intellectual stimulation

One of the main principles by which Paul Janssen led his research laboratory was 'continuous critical questioning'. He insisted that any data and results should be critically considered and that one should be ready to see new possibilities. This approach led to the creation of the antipsychotic drug haloperidol, a significant example of the laboratory's research principles in action. Paul Janssen noted: *'The human mind is like a parachute. It works best when it is open'* (Gurowitz, 2015). He also believed that 'research workers must stimulate one another intellectually' (Gurowitz, 2015). Much attention was paid to studying professional scientific publications in Paul Janssen's laboratory. An internal newsletter was regularly formed and distributed among scientists.

### Individualised consideration

The research centre of Paul Janssen was adapted to the needs of competent and motivated specialists, thanks to whom new drugs were created. The organisational structure of the laboratory was built on a horizontal type: not specialists for the laboratory, but the laboratory for specialists. Paul Janssen treated his employees with care, showed a sincere interest in them, knew their family problems, and supported their desire for self-development, believing that research must be their hobby. He exclaimed: 'What is nicer than being able to earn your living by practising your hobby?' (Gurowitz, 2015).

## 2.3 Types and characteristics of leaders

The evolution of leadership as a scientific direction has allowed the formation of types of leaders relevant to the business environment. Researchers of the ***trait approach*** of leadership sought to create a type of leader who can effectively influence their followers. Despite the variability of various leadership traits, most researchers agree that a true leader should possess emotional intelligence, responsibility, sociability, integrity, self-confidence, etc.

The transformational leadership theory presents the most precise and most understandable image of a leader. A ***transformational leader*** is a generator of change in an organisation, creates conditions for the development of followers, acts taking into account the system of internal values, and has the courage and the ability to cope with difficulties. According to Bass (1985, 1990), a transformational leader corresponds to people's ideas about an ideal leader who is a role model for them and inspires them to go 'the extra mile'.

The ***adaptive leader*** type, a widely applied concept in business, is distinct from the transformational leader. While transformational leaders may tend to dominate and sometimes 'overprotect' their followers, adaptive leaders focus on promoting people's adaptation to changing conditions and challenges. Heifetz et al. (2009) highlighted that in the case of complex adaptive challenges, the adaptive leader plays a crucial role in mobilising people to step out of their comfort zone, embrace new risks and problem-solving methods, and acquire fresh knowledge and skills.

One of the new types of leaders is an ***inclusive leader*** (Northouse, 2021), who promotes the creation of equal and fair conditions for all employees regardless of status differences, national and cultural characteristics, etc. An inclusive leader views multiculturalism, as well as EDI, as a strong point of the organisation. This perspective not only promotes innovation, creativity, and effective personnel involvement in achieving organisational goals but also inspires and motivates the workforce to push the boundaries of what's possible.

Bill George (2003) introduced the concept of the ***authentic leader*** in his book 'Authentic leadership: Rediscovering the secrets to creating lasting value'. This leader doesn't strive to mimic others but to understand and embrace their inner motives and values. As George describes, an authentic leader is driven by passion, puts their values into action, fosters enduring and fruitful relationships, shows compassion and care for people, and maintains a high level of self-discipline. Authentic leadership is a journey of personal growth shaped by life experiences, significant events, family relationships, and the unwavering commitment to self-discipline.

The ***servant leader*** type, proposed in the 1970s by Greenleaf (1970), is rooted in Christian ethics and morality. Like the transformational leader type, the servant leader demonstrates altruistic behaviour. The servant leader uses their influence to serve people and benefit society. In an organisation's context, this creates significant value for various stakeholders, be it clients, employees, partners, shareholders, or society.

Peter Drucker wrote about leaders as a generator of change. In his interpretation, they are a ***change leader*** whom the legendary scientist and management theorist found the only possibility of an organisation's long-term existence in modern conditions (Drucker & Maciariello, 2012).

Edwards Deming, a world-famous scientist and author of numerous works in quality management, is considered a ***leader as a coach and adviser*** (Neave, 1990). Such a leader tries to make work enjoyable for everyone, creates trust, helps improve, creates conditions for employees to use their skills and abilities, and listens and learns from others.

The next type of leader is the rare and exceptional ***level 5 leader***, as proposed by Jim Collins, the author of the bestsellers 'Built to Last' and 'Good to Great' (Collins, 2001). He suggests that these leaders are exceptional in achieving long-term results due to a paradoxical combination of outstanding personal and professional qualities.

The author attributes the exceptional ***professional will*** of the leader, namely:

- *Setting high standards for building a successful company.*
- *Demonstrating an unwavering desire to achieve outstanding long-term goals.*
- *Achieving desired results despite difficulties.*
- *Willingness to take full responsibility for unsatisfactory results.*

The ***personal humility*** that characterises level 5 leaders includes the following:

- *Modesty, does not seek wide fame and popularity.*
- *Acts calmly, not relying solely on charisma and personal charm.*
- *Realises his ambitious aspirations through the success of the company.*
- *Is ready to attribute the results to employees' merits, favourable external circumstances, and pure luck.*

**Food for thought:** ***What type of leader do you like the most? Explain why.***

**How it works in the pharmaceutical industry:** Description of the personal and professional qualities of a level 5 leader using the example of former CEO of Gilead Science, John C. Martin (Lou et al., 2022; Garabedian, 2021) (see Appendix B).

## Professional will

- *Setting high standards for building a successful company.*
  John C. Martin set high standards for developing innovative antiviral drugs, which allowed a small biopharmaceutical company, Gilead Science, to become a leader in the $120 billion biotech industry.
- *Demonstrating an unwavering desire to achieve outstanding long-term goals.*
  The successful launch of three drugs (for HIV infection, viral blindness in AIDS patients, and hepatitis B) under the leadership of Dr Martin contributed significantly to the long-term success of Gilead Science.

- *Achieving desired results despite difficulties.*
  Gilead Science, led by John C. Martin, spent years trying to develop the most effective drug for HIV infection. The effort was crowned with success: Atripla, a blockbuster drug, was created.
- *Willingness to take full responsibility for unsatisfactory results.*
  When Gilead Science was criticised for high prices for its hepatitis C drugs, Dr Martin took full responsibility for the problem. The company started cooperating with local manufacturers in developing countries to create generic medicines. It also donated antiviral medication for charity.

**Personal humility**

- *Modesty, does not seek wide fame and popularity.*
  John C. Martin was a modest, non-public person who did not appear on magazine covers or seek awards and recognition. At the same time, Harvard Business Review named him one of the most successful CEOs, along with Steve Jobs and Jeff Bezos.
- *Acts calmly, not relying solely on charisma and personal charm.*
  Dr Martin was a leader who listened more than he talked. He did not look or act like a charismatic leader, preferring to delegate representational functions, such as media appearances, to his team members.
- *Realises his ambitious aspirations through the success of the company.*
  John C. Martin's goal was to create a successful biotech company. To do so, he worked tirelessly to create new antiviral drugs and developed as a leader. For example, he received an MBA in marketing, which helped him manage the company more effectively.
- *Is ready to attribute the results to employees' merits, favourable external circumstances, and pure luck.*
  When asked about Gilead Science's success story and his leadership, Dr Martin emphasised the importance of teamwork and the ability to be flexible, make decisions quickly, and collaborate effectively with external stakeholders. He mentored his employees, setting an example of authentic leadership.

## 2.4 Conclusions

1 Leadership theories aim to find an answer to how a leader can effectively influence their followers to achieve the desired goal. There is no single and generally accepted classification of leadership theories. Still, they can be

divided into three clusters: focused on the personality of the leader, followers and the structure of tasks, and the relationship between the leader and followers. One of the prime examples of leadership theories in the pharmaceutical industry is the theory of adaptive leadership, which consists of motivating and focusing people on new complex challenges that often require changes in values, behaviour, and way of thinking.

2 Transformational leadership theory is one of the most popular, with contributions from various authors and researchers. A transformational leader creates conditions for achieving organisational results that exceed expectations through an effective combination of the following factors: idealised influence, inspiring motivation, intellectual stimulation, and individualised consideration. In business, transformational leadership effectively complements and improves transactional leadership, the essence of which is forming a mutually beneficial exchange between the organisation's leader and employees.
3 Leadership is an 'open book' inextricably linked to social and historical changes, technological progress, and other factors. This contributes to the emergence of new theories of leadership and leader types, such as the inclusive leader, which promotes the development of equity, diversity, and inclusion in an organisation. Researchers such as Bernard Bass, James Burns, Ronald Heifitz, Bill George, Jim Collins, Peter Drucker, Edwards Deming, and many others proposed their vision of the leader type.

## References


Aliekperova, N., & Aliekperov, A. (2023). Leadership traits as the basis for effective interaction between the leader and the team. *Journal of Leadership in Organizations*, 5(1). https://doi.org/10.22146/jlo.75402

Avolio, B.J. (1999). *Full Leadership Development: Building the Vital Forces in Organisations*. Thousand Oaks, CA: SAGE.

Bass, B.M. (1985). *Leadership and Performance Beyond Expectations*. New York, NY: Free Press.

Bass, B.M. (1990). From transactional to transformational leadership: Learning to share the vision. *Organisational Dynamics*, 18, 19–31. https://doi.org/10.1016/0090-2616(90)90061-S

Bass, B.M., (1998). *Transformational Leadership: Industry, Military, and Educational Impact*. Mahwah, NJ: Erlbaum.

Bass, B.M., & Avolio, B.J., (1994). *Improving Organisational Effectiveness through Transformational Leadership*. Thousand Oaks, CA: Sage.

Behrendt, P., Matz, S., & Göritz, A.S., (2017). An integrative model of leadership behaviour. *The Leadership Quarterly*, 28(1), 229–244. https://doi.org/10.1016/j.leaqua.2016.08.002

Blake, R.R., & Mouton, J.S., (1985). *The Managerial Grid III*. Houston, TX: Gulf.

Blanchard, K., Zigarmi, P., & Zigarmi, D., (2013). *Leadership and the One Minute Manager: Increasing Effectiveness through Situational Leadership II*. New York, NY: William Morrow.

Burns, J.M., (1978). *Leadership*. New York, NY: Harper & Row.

Burns, J.M., (2003). *Transforming Leadership: A New Pursuit of Happiness*. New York, NY: Atlantic Monthly Pr.

Collins, J., (2001). Level 5 leadership: The triumph of humility and fierce resolve. *Harvard Business Review*, 79(1), 66–175.

Dansereau, F., Graen, G.B., & Haga, W., (1975). A vertical dyad linkage approach to leadership in formal organisations. *Organisational Behavior and Human Performance*, 13, 46–78. http://dx.doi.org/10.1016/0030-5073(75)90005-7

Drucker, P., & Maciariello, J., (2012). *The Daily Drucker: 366 Days of Insight and Motivation for Getting the Right Things Done*. Russian eds. M.: Mann, Ivanov and Ferber. New York: HarperBusiness.

Fiedler, F., (1967). *A Theory of Leadership Effectiveness*. New York, NY: McGraw-Hill.

Garabedian, C., (2021). The Glory of John Martin: An Understated Leader Who Built a Biotech Powerhouse. Timmerman Report, 5 April 2021. Available from: https://timmermanreport.com/2021/04/the-glory-of-john-martin-an-understated-leader-who-built-a-biotech-powerhouse/ [Accessed 15 December 2023].

George, B., (2003). *Authentic Leadership: Rediscovering the Secrets to Creating Lasting Value*. San Francisco, CA: Jossey-Bass.

Graen, G.B., & Cashman, J., (1975). A role-making model of leadership in formal organisations: A developmental approach. In J.G. Hunt & L.L. Larson (Eds.), *Leadership Frontiers* (pp. 143–166). Kent, OH: Kent State University Press.

Greenleaf, R.K., (1970). *The Servant as Leader*. Westfield, IN: Greenleaf Center for Servant Leadership.

Gulland, A., (2020). Pfizer chief: vaccine success was down to 'thinking big'. *The Telegraph*, 8 December 2020. Available from: https://www.telegraph.co.uk/global-health/science-and-disease/pfizer-chief-vaccine-success-thinking-big/ [Accessed 23 December 2023].

Gurowitz, M., (2015). The legacy of Dr. Paul Janssen: How a "funny idea" helped change the course of modern medicine. *Johnson & Johnson*, 11 September 2015. Available from: https://www.jnj.com/the-legacy-of-dr-paul-janssen-how-a-funny-idea-helped-change-the-course-of-modern-medicine [Accessed 11 December 2023].

Heifetz, R.A., (1994). *Leadership without Easy Answers*. Cambridge, MA: Belknap Press.

Heifetz, R.A., Grashow, A., & Linsky, M., (2009). *The Practice of Adaptive Leadership: Tools and Tactics for Changing Your Organisation and the World*. Boston, MA: Harvard Business School Press.

Hemphill, J.K., & Coons, A.E., (1957). Development of the leader behavior description questionnaire. In R.M. Stogdill & A.E. Coons (Eds.), *Leader Behavior: Its Description and Measurement (Research Monograph No. 88)*. Columbus: The Ohio State University, Bureau of Business Research.

Hersey, P., & Blanchard, K.H., (1996). Great ideas revisited: Revisiting the life-cycle theory of leadership. *Training & Development Journal*, 50(1), 42.

House, R.J., & Mitchell, R.R., (1974). Path-goal theory of leadership. *Journal of Contemporary Business*, 3, 81–97.

Katz, R.L., (1955). Skills of an effective administrator. *Harvard Business Review*, 33(1), 33–42.

Lewi, P.J., & Smith, A., (2007). Successful pharmaceutical discovery: Paul Janssen's concept of drug research. *R&D Management*, 37(4), 355–362. https://doi.org/10.1111/j.1467-9310.2007.00481.x

Likert, R., (1961). *New Patterns of Management*. New York, NY: McGraw-Hill.

Likert, R., (1967). *The Human Organisation: Its Management and Value*. New York, NY: McGraw-Hill.

Lou, L.L., Flood, A., Yang, T., & Whitley, R.J., (2022). Commentary: John C. Martin (1951–2021). *Antiviral Therapy*, 27(2). https://journals.sagepub.com/doi/full/10.1177/13596535211067895

Mumford, M.D., Zaccaro, S.J., Connelly, M.S., & Marks, M.A., (2000). Leadership skills: Conclusions and future directions. *The Leadership Quarterly*, 11(1), 155–170. https://doi.org/10.1016/S1048-9843(99)00047-8

National Journal, (n.d.). *Business leaders: Albert Bourla*. National Journal. Available from: https://go.nationaljournal.com/rs/556-YEE-969/images/BusinessLeaders_Albert_Bourla.pdf [Accessed 10 August 2024].

Neave, H.R., (1990). *The Deming Dimension*. Knoxville, TN: SPC Press.

Northouse, P.G., (2021). *Leadership: Theory and Practice*. 9th edition. Los Angeles, CA: Sage Publications.

# 3 Traits and skills of leaders in the pharmaceutical industry

## 3.1 Personal traits of leaders

One of the most famous researchers of the trait approach in leadership was Ralph Stogdill, who, in 1948, based on an analysis of literary sources, identified the most optimal traits, the possession of which makes an ordinary person a leader. Later, in 1974, Stogdill revised and changed the leadership qualities list. In addition, sets of leadership traits were proposed by researchers (Table 3.1) (Aliekperova & Aliekperov, 2023).

*Table 3.1* Bibliometric research of leadership traits

| *Researchers* | *Year* | *Traits* |
|---|---|---|
| Stogdill | 1948 | Intelligence, alertness, insight, responsibility, initiative, persistence, self-confidence, sociability |
| Mann | 1959 | Intelligence, masculinity, adjustment, dominance, extraversion, conservatism |
| Stogdill | 1974 | Achievement, persistence, insight, initiative, self-confidence, responsibility, cooperativeness, tolerance, influence, sociability |
| Lord, de Vader, and Alliger | 1986 | Intelligence, masculinity, dominance, stress tolerance, high energy level, self-confidence, integrity, emotional maturity |
| Kirkpatrick and Locke | 1991 | Cognitive ability, motivation, drive, integrity, confidence, task knowledge |
| Yukl and Van Fleet | 1992 | Emotional maturity, integrity, self-confidence, high energy level, stress tolerance |
| House and Aditya | 1997 | Achievement motivation, prosocial influence motivation, adjustment, self-confidence |
| Yukl | 1998 | Energy level and stress tolerance, self-confidence, emotional maturity, internal locus of control, personality integrity, socialised power motivation, achievement orientation, low need for affiliation |
| Zaccaro, Kemp, and Bader | 2004 | Cognitive ability, extraversion, consciousness, emotional stability, openness, agreeableness, motivation, self-monitoring, emotional intelligence, problem-solving, emotional stability |

DOI: 10.4324/9781003617266-4

Despite the subjectivity in defining leadership qualities in various studies, several common clusters can be identified: a leader must be intelligent; a leader must be emotionally stable; a leader must be able to interact with people; a leader must motivate and be able to influence people; a leader must comply with ethical standards; a leader must strive to achieve the target goals; and a leader must be responsible and confident in their actions (Aliekperova & Aliekperov, 2023).

### *Cluster 1 – A leader must be intelligent*

A leader's ***intelligence*** *or* ***cognitive abilities*** are traits without which a person is unlikely to become a leader and influence others. To lead in an organisation, it is necessary to be able to analyse information and take into account the influence of various factors, which requires not only a high level of intelligence but also the constant development of intellectual competencies. The Cambridge Dictionary (n.d.) defines intelligence as 'the ability to learn, understand, and make judgments'.

However, their presence does not guarantee success despite the importance of a leader's cognitive abilities. For example, IQ allows us to identify a person's genetic predisposition to logical thinking, a penchant for specific sciences, etc. However, there is no direct relationship between a leader's performance and IQ. In the 1920s, psychologist Lewis Terman began an experiment to determine the relationship between children's intelligence and their living conditions (Terman, 2021). In 1956, the experiment continued, leading to the conclusion that a person's intellectual abilities play an important, but not decisive, role in achieving success. However, an intellectually developed person understands the importance of self-development for success, so intelligence is an essential quality of a leader.

### *Cluster 2 – A leader must be emotionally stable*

An authentic leader tries to analyse their thoughts, statements, and actions adequately and, if necessary, correct them. They understand that working with people to resolve possible conflict situations requires ***self-monitoring (emotional maturity)*** from the leader. Former CEO of Novartis, Daniel Vasella, pointed out the need for an advisor (partner, friend) who can be completely trusted, understands, supports, and allows the leader to maintain the necessary 'emotional ballast' (Kirkland, 2012). It is worth citing the famous statement by Lao Tzu: 'Mastering others is strength; mastering yourself is true power'.

Self-monitoring is associated with such a trait as ***emotional intelligence***, which implies the leader's ability to recognise and manage their emotions, especially negative ones, such as fear, anger, and despair. Yukl (1998, p. 152) emphasised that 'leaders with a high level of emotional intelligence are more capable of solving complex problems, planning how to use their time effectively, adapting their behaviour to the situation, and managing crises'. This trait allows leaders to maintain emotional stability when making decisions and interacting with team members, thereby enhancing their leadership effectiveness.

### *Cluster 3 – A leader must be able to interact with people*

To clearly and understandably convey information about the goals and vision of the organisation's development, leaders should possess ***sociability***, which allows them to effectively influence their followers, receive feedback, and understand the mood and motivation of people. Leaders with interpersonal skills can build effective relationships with their followers.

The critical leadership trait that influences the interaction process between a leader and followers is ***social intelligence***, namely the ability to recognise and manage the emotions of others. Yukl (1998) states that social intelligence helps leaders choose appropriate behaviour when interacting with people. The mechanism for recognising the emotions of others is similar to identifying one's own emotions. In this case, non-verbal communication, such as gestures, facial expressions, voice, body position, etc., plays a significant role. Social intelligence involves developing skills such as active listening, the ability to conclude from the information received, asking open questions, paraphrasing, showing empathy, and being a moderator in conflict situations.

### *Cluster 4 – A leader must motivate and be able to influence people*

According to Bass (1990), the main task of inspiration is to motivate people to make every effort to achieve shared goals. The ***ability to inspire*** means encouraging employees to create value at three levels: for employees, the company, and society. This is how Pfizer CEO Albert Bourla inspired his team by setting them the goal of creating an effective vaccine against COVID-19 in the shortest possible time. Not only the employees were inspired by an ambitious goal that allowed them to implement their knowledge and skills to receive recognition and the desired reward, but they also felt a deep sense of pride in being part of a successful and socially oriented organisation. Antoine de Saint Exupéry noted: 'If you want to build a ship, don't drum up people to collect wood and don't assign them tasks and work, but rather teach them to long for the endless immensity of the sea'.

The trait that enables a leader to inspire people to take the actions necessary to achieve a set goal is ***charisma.*** House, the author of the theory of the charismatic leader, connects the personal characteristics of a charismatic leader with their ability to influence people. The author names trust in the leader, devotion to their ideas, and emotional involvement among the effects that affect followers (Northouse, 2021). It is worth noting that charisma is not external masculinity and dominance but internal positive energy that the leader shares with others. According to Bass (1990), charisma is vital for a leader to serve as a role model for followers and help them improve. However, Kirkpatrick and Locke (1991) noted that charisma may not be very important for effective leadership. Additionally, charisma is not included in the list of leadership traits formulated by researchers using the trait approach (see Table 3.1). This omission is mainly because charisma can lead to negative consequences without moral and ethical guidelines. However, if a leader is focused on achieving positive results and acts according to ethical standards, charisma can help them achieve their goals.

### *Cluster 5 – A leader must comply with ethical standards*

***Integrity*** is one of the leadership qualities based on compliance with ethical standards. Jack Welch, the legendary CEO of General Electric, noted that integrity is the most essential value and emphasised, 'We never had a corporate meeting where I didn't emphasise integrity in my closing remark' (Weinberger, 2010). Integrity significantly impacts the leader's followers, forming trust in their vision for the organisation's development.

### *Cluster 6 – A leader must strive to achieve the target goals*

Drucker (2008) noted that the results determine a leader's effectiveness. Due to such a trait as ***effectiveness (achievement)***, the leader's efforts aim to obtain results that create value for the company and its business. For a business leader, effectiveness is also determined by the following criteria: consistency in achieving goals, sustainable development of the organisation, and creating conditions for the emergence of new leaders. The task of an effective leader is to achieve the set goals not for personal ambitions but for the long-term and sustainable development of the company.

Effectiveness is directly related to leadership traits, such as the ***ability to set goals (vision).*** Thus, John C. Martin chose the creation of innovative antiviral drugs as a long-term goal of the biopharmaceutical company Gilead Science, Daniel Vasella set the development and production of innovative biological medicines and biosimilars for the treatment of rare diseases as his goal, Paul Janssen aimed for the synthesis of new chemical compounds for the creation of new drugs, and Charles Walgreen III aspired to create a leading pharmacy chain in the US market.

To achieve goals, a leadership trait such as ***passion (drive)*** plays a significant role. However, passion for a business leader is not a set of random chaotic actions caused by the influence of emotions but purposeful efforts supported by a strong desire to achieve the set goal. Passion is a 'fuel' that gives the leader the energy to implement the plan and also inspires others to follow suit. This trait also correlates with ***persistence (determination)*** in achieving goals. As Daniel Vasella noted: 'After diagnosing a situation, you have to act diligently and often quickly' (Harvard Business School, 2003).

### *Cluster 7 – A leader must be responsible and confident in their actions*

The company's leader must bear full ***responsibility*** for all business processes since management decisions directly affect employees, clients, and other stakeholders. Jim Collins (2001) noted that a true leader 'looks in the mirror' regarding responsibility for unsatisfactory results and, conversely, 'looks out the window' when the organisation succeeds.

A leader must have ***self-confidence*** to achieve goals, obtain the necessary results, and inspire team members. If a leader doubts the correctness of the decisions made and demonstrates uncertainty, followers will trust the leader less, and their motivation to achieve goals will decrease.

The list of leadership traits can be expanded to include the ***ability to change (change intelligence), the ability to take risks, the pursuit of new knowledge, the love of freedom,*** etc. (Aliekperova & Aliekperov, 2023). For instance, the love of freedom, a trait not mentioned in the list of leadership traits proposed by various researchers, is a crucial quality for a business leader. This trait implies responsibility for not only the consequences of decisions made but also the provision of the necessary level of freedom for employees.

It is crucial to understand that a leader's list of traits that lead to an organisation's successful development is significantly influenced by a myriad of external factors. These factors, including situations and relationships with followers, are pivotal in shaping leadership traits. It is imperative to independently determine what traits should be developed to remain a leader for an extended period.

**Food for thought:** ***Which leadership traits do you consider most essential?***

**How it works in the pharmaceutical industry:** Description of the personal leadership traits of the founder of Janssen Pharmaceutica, Paul Janssen (Lewi & Smith, 2007) (Appendix A).

### Cluster 1 – A leader must be intelligent

Paul Janssen's exceptional education in medicine, a testament to his ***intelligence (cognitive abilities)***, was just the beginning of his journey. His expertise in chemical synthesis and pharmacology, where he became an undisputed expert, set him apart in the scientific community. He was actively involved in scientific activities, developed professionally throughout his life, had a fantastic ability to visualise the structures of the molecules of the compounds he studied, was an avid chess player, played the piano, etc.

### Cluster 2 – A leader must be emotionally stable

Paul Janssen, one of the most productive inventors, dedicated his life to creating new drugs. His work exemplifies productive scientific research characteristics involving systematicity, concentration, patience, and persistence, characterising high ***self-monitoring (emotional maturity)***. Janssen's use of ***emotional intelligence*** to cope with inevitable difficulties in the research process maintained his emotional stability and ensured long-term leadership.

### Cluster 3 – A leader must be able to interact with people

The organisational structure of the laboratory, built on a horizontal type with minimised bureaucratic influence, was a testament to Dr Paul Janssen's leadership. His ***sociability***, demonstrated through his participation in scientific events and interactions with various stakeholders, played a significant role in fostering trusting professional relationships with his employees. Dr Paul's ***social intelligence*** manifested in the ability to effectively motivate and support his employees, inspire them in times of difficulties and uncertainty, be an attentive interlocutor, moderate various conflict situations, etc.

### Cluster 4 – A leader must motivate and be able to influence people

Paul Janssen's leadership was characterised by his ***ability to inspire*** his employees, first and foremost, by his example. His unwavering desire to do what he loved – to create innovative medicines – was a testament to his passion. He also selected people with similar values, recognising the importance of shared values in inspiring a team. These individuals were inspired by their research projects, involvement in a successful company, and the opportunity to benefit people. According to colleagues, Dr Paul had such a leadership trait as ***charisma*** due to his sincere interest in people, curiosity, and constant desire to learn and discover new things.

## Cluster 5 – A leader must comply with ethical standards

The famous phrase of Paul Janssen, 'The patients are waiting' (Gurowitz, 2015), characterises his life philosophy, which is based on serving people and observing moral and ethical principles. As a leader, Paul Janssen demonstrated ***integrity*** by building trusting relationships with his employees. But more than that, he fostered a sense of unity and collaboration, bringing professionals with similar values and motivations together.

## Cluster 6 – A leader must strive to achieve the target goals

Paul Janssen's professional career was marked by his ***effectiveness (achievement).*** Under his leadership, about 80 innovative drugs were developed, some recognised by the WHO as essential, and he held over 100 patents. Janssen's leadership also led to the success of one of the most financially successful research centres and contributed significantly to the development of science in the fields of pharmacology, biochemistry, toxicology, etc. As a student, Janssen's clear ***vision*** was evident in his decision to devote his life to pharmaceuticals. At 27, he turned this vision into reality, founding his company, Janssen Pharmaceutica, which impacted the pharmaceutical industry by developing and testing new chemical compounds. Thanks to such traits as ***passion***, Paul Janssen steadily moved towards achieving the desired goal – creating new drugs. He expected the same passion for achieving the desired result and the courage to follow his dream from his employees. Paul Janssen's ***persistence, or determination***, was not just a personal trait but a driving force behind the creation of new drugs. This was reflected in his attitude towards research projects in the laboratory, from forming the project concept as an idea to publishing a scientific article with the research results (obtaining a patent and launching a new drug on the market).

**Cluster 7 – A leader must be responsible and confident in their actions**

Paul Janssen took full ***responsibility*** for his decisions, some of which required courage and risk. For example, despite unfavourable market forecasts, he allowed researchers from the former Belgian colony to pursue their scientific projects. As a result, blockbuster drugs such as mebendazole and miconazole entered the market. Dr Paul demonstrated such a leadership trait as ***self-confidence*** throughout his life. His belief in himself, his mission, and his team led to millions of people receiving access to effective drug therapy.

## 3.2 Skills approach in leadership

Leadership skills and types of intellectual competencies (emotional intelligence/social intelligence/change intelligence) are improved in practical activities in situations of challenges and uncertainties that require new management approaches.

***The skills approach*** introduced by Robert Katz in his article ‘Skills of an Effective Administrator’ in the Harvard Business Review in 1955 is a universally applicable framework for understanding and developing managerial skills (Katz, 1955). Katz’s work categorises these skills into technical, human, and conceptual. The higher the management level, the more in-demand conceptual skills are; conversely, technical skills will be most relevant at a lower management level. It is worth noting that, according to the author, human skills are essential at all levels of management: top management, middle management, and supervisory management. This approach is relevant and necessary for all managers, regardless of their roles or industries.

***Technical skills*** for a leader are the presence of specialised competencies, knowledge of tools and technologies, and the use of analytical skills to solve technical problems. All influential leaders in the pharmaceutical industry had specialised education and relevant professional competencies (medicine, pharmacy, chemistry, etc.) (see Appendixes A–I). These skills allowed them to form a vision of the company’s development and set a standard of professionalism for their employees. More importantly, they enabled these leaders to make effective management decisions, significantly contributing to the business’s success.

***Human skills***, the foundation of universal leadership, inspire growth and development in building effective relationships and achieving organisational goals. As per Bass’s transformational theory of leadership, the ability to articulate the vision and values of the organisation, foster trust, inspire goal achievement, and develop the intellectual potential of followers leads to performance ‘beyond expectation’.

According to Katz, ***conceptual skills*** are the bedrock of top management, closely followed by human skills. Conceptual skills involve manipulating ideas and concepts to form a vision and strategy for an organisation's growth. For a leader in the pharmaceutical industry, developing these skills means not only mastering specialised competencies but also understanding the fundamental principles of business and the intricacies of long-term company development.

The skills approach was further developed after Mumford and his colleagues developed ***a skill-based model of leadership*** (Mumford et al., 2000). This model draws attention to the fact that a leader's effectiveness depends on developing and successfully implementing leadership competencies in solving management problems (see Figure 3.1).

The authors present general/crystallised cognitive abilities, motivation, and personality as ***individual attributes***. General cognitive abilities, such as the innate ability to perceive and analyse information, creative thinking, and memory, are necessary for leaders. Crystallised cognitive abilities or acquired skills like working with complex information systems can lead to desirable organisational goals. Motivation, the willingness to solve organisational issues, influence others, and create value for stakeholders, is a key driver of productivity. Lastly, personality has practical implications for long-lasting leadership.

***Competencies*** include problem-solving skills, social judgment skills, and knowledge. Problem-solving skills are a leader's ability to solve new, unstructured problems. On the other hand, social judgment skills enable a leader to understand and manage people and the functioning of social systems. Such competency as knowledge implies that a leader has accumulated information and mental structures necessary for structuring information.

***Leadership outcomes*** include effective problem-solving and performance. For effective problem-solving, a leader must use a creative, unique approach 'beyond existing patterns and standards', leading to performance – implementing a problem solution optimally and effectively. Thus, John C. Martin set himself the goal to solve the following problem: to develop an effective drug for treating HIV infection which could replace the drug cocktails. For

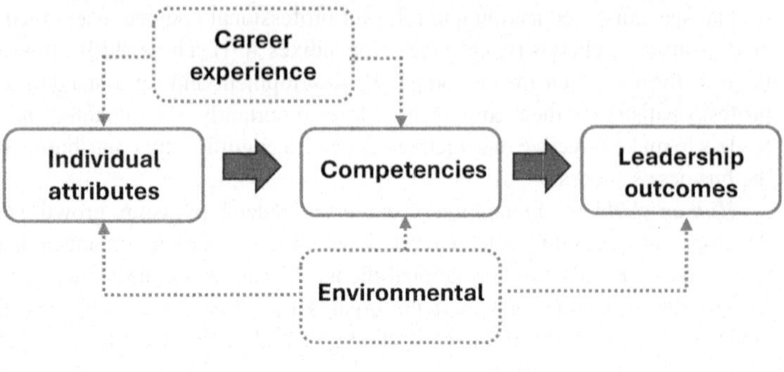


*Figure 3.1* Components of a skill-based model of leadership.

example, patients were forced to take about 20 different medications per day, both with and without food, which significantly hindered compliance and the effectiveness of treatment. Dr Martin achieved the desired performance: the vision of 'one pill, once a day' was realised. The drug Atripla, which entered the market in 2006, became the most prescribed drug for HIV-infected patients in the United States, with sales of about $2 billion per year (Yang et al., 2022).

According to the model of Mumford and colleagues, a leader's individual attributes and competencies are influenced by ***career experience.*** The experience that a leader acquires during their professional career influences the quality of knowledge and skills in solving complex and ambitious tasks.

The development of leadership qualities, competencies, and desired outcomes depends on ***environmental influence***, both internal factors – resources, technologies, and employee competencies – and external ones – competition, market development, economic situation, social processes, technological progress, etc. A leader in the pharmaceutical industry will only be able to implement the desired vision of the company's development with the necessary financial resources, availability of material and technical base, and competent and motivated specialists.

It is worth noting that, unlike Katz's three-skill approach, the skills model of Mumford and colleagues is complex, combining trait and skills approaches and factors that influence a leader's effectiveness in achieving desired leadership outcomes.

**Food for thought: *Which skills influence leadership outcomes most?***

**How it works in the pharmaceutical industry:** Description of leadership skills of former CEO Gilead Science John C. Martin by Katz's three-skill approach (Lou et al., 2022; Garabedian, 2021) (Appendix B).

### Technical skills

John C. Martin received his BS in chemical engineering and a PhD in organic chemistry from the University of Chicago. He then developed his specialised skills as a laboratory researcher and R&D team leader. The technical skills Martin acquired allowed him to formulate the vision for Gilead Science, aimed at creating innovative antiviral drugs to treat various diseases. His expertise and specialised professional experience contributed to effective management decisions and the successful development of Gilead Science.

**Human skills**

John C. Martin, as a leader, was well aware of the importance of effective interaction with people. He mentored his team members, inspiring, guiding, and supporting their aspirations to develop and improve their professional skills. He maintained close contact with leading scientists, physicians, and the patient community. In this way, Gilead Science not only strengthened beneficial interactions with various stakeholders but also received feedback on the effectiveness of drug therapy. This also allowed the company to adhere to its core value of being focused on the needs of patients.

**Conceptual skills**

As soon as John C. Martin became CEO of the biopharmaceutical company Gilead Science, he immediately determined the direction of the company's development. The emphasis was on creating innovative antiviral drugs, considering patients' needs. To successfully lead the company, John C. Martin decided to gain new business skills, particularly an MBA in marketing. John C. Martin was a man of ideas, which he implemented with persistence and determination; for example, he successfully implemented the concept of 'one pill, once a day' to create innovative drug therapy for HIV-infected patients.

## 3.3 System thinking in pharmaceutical leadership

As an intellectual competence, ***systems thinking*** empowers a leader to successfully develop an organisation, focusing on achieving both short-term and long-term goals. It is based on the principles of holism, which view the whole as more than the sum of its parts, but as a system of interconnected and cooperating elements. The adaptive leadership theory assumes that a leader possesses systems thinking skills, particularly the ability to 'get on the balcony'. This metaphorical action allows a leader to gain a comprehensive view of the organisation, understanding how its parts are integrated and interact to achieve goals. According to Katz's three-skill approach, a leader's conceptual skills also imply systems thinking skills, enabling them to form a vision and strategy for the organisation's development, considering the interrelation of functional processes.

According to Meadows (2008, p. 188), a ***system*** is 'a set of elements or parts that is coherently organised and interconnected in a pattern or structure that produces a characteristic set of behaviours, often classified as its 'function' or 'purpose'.

An organisation, a division of an organisation, or an organisational project can also be considered a system. For example, a system is not only a big pharmaceutical corporation such as Novartis or Pfizer but also the Paul Janssen Research Center as a division of the global company Johnson & Johnson or the MDP, organised by the pharmaceutical company Merck.

According to Meadows (2008), a system consists of the following elements: parts, interrelation or interconnection of parts, and purpose (function).

In an organisation, ***parts*** of the system can be considered as its divisions or people working in these divisions. Some parts of the system can be key as they affect the functioning of the entire system. For example, the leader of an organisation, as part of a system, can be considered the most crucial part of the system since they determine the vision for the development of the company and its further transformation.

The following characteristic of the system is the ***interrelation and interconnection*** of its parts. Thus, the successful launch of a new drug on the market depends on each department, whether it is R&D, manufacturing, or marketing. For example, the safety and effectiveness of an API can be confirmed by the results of preclinical and clinical trials. However, the technology of mass production or the marketing strategy of promotion can be imperfect. As a result, patients do not have access to effective drug therapy, and the company faces significant losses. To avoid this, the departments must interact with each other productively. Information plays a vital role in this process. Meadows (2008, p. 14) noted that 'information holds systems together and plays a great role in determining how they operate'. Wheatley (2006, p. 160) emphasised that 'information is a dynamic, changing element, taking centre stage', without which the system cannot fully function. 'Poor communication', according to Wheatley (2006), is one of the most common problems employees face in an organisation. The leader's task is crucial in creating conditions for effective organisational communication, especially during organisational changes.

***Purpose*** is the unifying and motivating element of the organisation as a system. According to Ackoff et al. (2010), successful implementation of systems thinking depends on how managers understand the common ground between the various parts of the organisation and how they can act together. An organisation's unifying and motivating purpose is usually the vision, which is an image of the company's future and what it strives to become. Vision allows the integration of the employees' efforts, knowledge, and intelligence into the organisation and becomes the driving force of its development (Bratianu & Balanescu, 2008). As a rule, vision reflects the values and motivation of the leader.

Systems thinking skills allow a leader to transform an organisation effectively. However, it's important to note that implementing systems thinking in an organisation can be challenging. It assumes that a change in one part of the system should entail changes in others. Ackoff (1999) noted that a change in one part that does not lead to a change in the whole can have negative consequences. He illustrated this concept with the example of replacing a Hyundai's engine with a Rolls Royce engine, which could render the car unusable. Senge (1990) emphasised that systems thinking is aimed at seeing patterns of change rather than snapshots. A leader with systems thinking realises that the organisational change process should affect all functional processes. For this, all departments and employees in the organisation must effectively interact with each other, exchange information, and acquire new knowledge and skills. For example, the digital transformation of a modern customer-oriented organisation requires changes at all levels, be it improving communications and business processes within the organisation and externally, in particular, the use of integrated marketing communications when interacting with clients. The leader's role in the organisational change process is vital (see Section 8.3).

Systems thinking is not just a cognitive, intellectual competence of a leader that promotes productive results; it is a perspective, a language, and a set of tools. It is a language that includes tools like feedback loops, complexity, hierarchies, self-organisation, etc. (Monat & Gannon, 2015). For example, the Iceberg Model, which explains the relationship between visible events and mental models of behaviour, is used to understand the phenomenon of organisational culture. For organisations, including pharmaceutical ones, systems thinking is the key to addressing everyday business problems (Monat, 2020).

**Food for thought:** ***How are the intelligence competencies of a leader connected with system thinking?***

**How it works in the pharmaceutical industry:** A description of the systems thinking elements using the example of Sandostatin launch to the market under the leadership of Daniel Vasella (Encyclopedia.com, n.d.) (Appendix E).

## Parts of system

The ***system*** is a project for developing, researching, producing, and promoting an anticancer drug to the pharmaceutical market under the leadership of Daniel Vasella. The ***parts*** of this system are separate departments responsible for development, research, production, marketing, and the employees working in these departments. Daniel Vasella, as the project leader, is also part of this system.

### Interrelation and interconnection of system parts

Daniel Vasella was the first at Sandoz to unite the activities of departments, establishing effective ***interconnection*** between them. Chemists, clinicians, technologists, and marketers began to work not in isolation, as before, but together. Employees of various departments freely exchanged information and solved problems that arose. This enabled avoiding the risks and issues that product managers had previously encountered while launching new medications.

### Purpose

The unifying and motivating ***purpose*** of the project was the successful launch of Sandostatin, which integrated the efforts, knowledge, and skills of all employees involved in development, testing, production, and marketing. This goal not only made innovative drug therapy available to patients but also led to a significant financial impact. By 2001, Sandostatin sales reached $486 million, a clear indicator of the project's success.

## 3.4 Conclusions

1 The list of leadership traits is not universal; in many ways, it is subjective. However, it is possible to identify clusters that define vital leadership traits, including intelligence, responsibility, the ability to motivate and influence followers, communicate effectively, achieve goals, be emotionally stable, demonstrate self-confidence, and adhere to moral and ethical principles. A business leader can independently determine the traits that need to be developed for successful and long-term leadership of the organisation.
2 Leadership skills are acquired and developed throughout a professional career and are improved in situations of challenges and uncertainty. According to Katz's skills approach, the most important leadership skills are conceptual skills, which imply the ability to work with ideas and concepts, for example, to develop an organisation's development strategy. Human skills are also necessary, enabling leaders to effectively understand and work with people. A skill-based model of leadership notes that successful leadership outcomes depend not only on the leader's competencies but also on their personal qualities and characteristics, unique career experience, and internal and external factors that influence the achievement of organisational goals.

3 Systems thinking is an essential intellectual competence of a leader. It provides a clear framework for holistically managing the system, including its parts, interrelations, and motivating purpose. A leader with systems thinking skills understands that effective changes necessitate the transformation of all parts of the system, paving the way for the organisation's sustainable development with a sense of certainty and security.

## References

Ackoff, R., (1999). *A Lifetime of System Thinking.* The system thinkers [online], 10(5).

Ackoff, R., Addison, H., & Carey, A., (2010). *Systems Thinking for Curious Managers.* Charmouth: Triarchy Press.

Aliekperova, N., & Aliekperov, A., (2023). Leadership traits as the basis for effective interaction between the leader and the team. *Journal of Leadership in Organizations,* 5(1). https://doi.org/10.22146/jlo.75402

Bass, B.M., (1990). From transactional to transformational leadership: Learning to share the vision. *Organisational Dynamics,* 18, 19–31. https://doi.org/10.1016/0090-2616(90)90061-S

Bratianu, C., & Balanescu, G., (2008). Vision, leadership and strategic management. *Management & Marketing,* 3(1), 19–38.

Cambridge Dictionary, (n.d.). *Meaning of intelligence in English* [online]. Cambridge Dictionary. Available from: https://dictionary.cambridge.org/dictionary/english/intelligence [Accessed 12 January 2024].

Collins, J., (2001). *Good to Great.* London: Random House Business Books.

Drucker, P., (2008). *The Effective Executive.* New York: Harper Business.

Encyclopedia.com, (n.d.). *Vasella, Daniel 1953– International Directory of Business Biographies.* Encyclopedia.com [online]. Available from: https://www.encyclopedia.com/economics/news-wires-white-papers-and-books/vasella-daniel-1953 [Accessed 15 January 2024].

Garabedian, C., (2021). The glory of John Martin: An understated leader who built a biotech powerhouse. *Timmerman Report* [online], 5 April 2021. Available from: https://timmermanreport.com/2021/04/the-glory-of-john-martin-an-understated-leader-who-built-a-biotech-powerhouse/ [Accessed 15 December 2023].

Gurowitz, M., (2015). The legacy of Dr. Paul Janssen: How a "funny idea" helped change the course of modern medicine. *Johnson & Johnson* [online], 11 September 2015. Available from: https://www.jnj.com/the-legacy-of-dr-paul-janssen-how-a-funny-idea-helped-change-the-course-of-modern-medicine [Accessed 11 December 2023].

Harvard Business School, (2003). *Daniel L. Vasella, M.D. 2003 Alumni Achievement Award Recipient* [online]. Harvard Business School. Available from: https://www.alumni.hbs.edu/stories/Pages/story-bulletin.aspx?num=2019 [Accessed 11 February 2024].

Katz, R.L., (1955). Skills of an effective administrator. *Harvard Business Review,* 33(1), 33–42.

Kirkland, R., (2012). *Leading in the 21st century: An interview with Daniel Vasella.* [online]. McKinsey & Company. Available from: https://www.mckinsey.com/~/media/McKinsey/Featured%20Insights/Leading%20in%20the%2021st%20Century/An%20interview%20with%20Daniel%20Vasella/Daniel_Vasella.pdf [Accessed 4 December 2023].

Kirkpatrick, S.A., & Locke, E.A., (1991). Leadership: Do traits matter? *Academy of Management Executive*, 5(2), 48–60. https://doi.org/10.5465/ame.1991.4274679

Lewi, P.J., & Smith, A., (2007). Successful pharmaceutical discovery: Paul Janssen's concept of drug research. *R&D Management*, 37(4), 355–362. https://doi.org/10.1111/j.1467-9310.2007.00481.x

Lou, L.L., Flood, A., Yang, T., & Whitley, R.J., (2022). Commentary: John C. Martin (1951–2021). *Antiviral Therapy*, 27(2). https://journals.sagepub.com/doi/full/10.1177/13596535211067895

Meadows, D.H., (2008). *Thinking in Systems: A Primer*. London: Earthscan.

Monat, J.P., (2020). *Practical Applications of Systems Thinking to Everyday Life*. Boca Raton, FL: CRC Press.

Monat, J.P., & Gannon, T.F., (2015). What is systems thinking? A review of selected literature plus recommendations. *American Journal of Systems Science*, 4, 11–26. doi: http://article.sapub.org/10.5923.j.ajss.20150401.02.html

Mumford, M.D., Zaccaro, S.J., Connelly, M.S., & Marks, M.A., (2000). Leadership skills: Conclusions and future directions. *The Leadership Quarterly*, 11(1), 155–170. https://doi.org/10.1016/S1048-9843(99)00047-8

Northouse, P.G., (2021). *Leadership: Theory and Practice*. 9th edition. Los Angeles, CA: Sage Publications.

Senge, P., (1990). *The Fifth Discipline: The Art and Practice of the Learning Organization*. New York: Doubleday/Currency.

Terman, L., (2021). *Genetic Studies of Genius: The Terman Study*. Cambridge: Cambridge University Press.

Weinberger, D., (2010). The American leader's love affair with hierarchy. *Harvard Business Review* [online], 29 October 2010. Available from: https://hbr.org/2010/10/the-american-leaders-love-affa [Accessed 18 February 2024].

Wheatley, M., (2006). *Leadership and the New Science: Discovering Order in a Chaotic World*. San Francisco, CA: Berrett-Koehler Publishers.

Yang, H., Li, X., & Zhu, X., (2022). Transformational leadership and its role in organizational innovation: A systematic review. *Leadership Studies Quarterly*, 8(3), 124–140. https://doi.org/10.3390/su15075756

Yukl, G., (1998). *Leadership in Organizations*. Upper Saddle River, NJ: Prentice Hall.

# 4 Leadership styles and team leadership in the pharmaceutical industry

## 4.1 Leadership styles of leaders

The behavioural approach in leadership, and subsequently the situational approach, allowed us to form the main leadership styles that will enable us to achieve organisational goals effectively. One of the first to classify leadership styles was the German and later American social psychologist Kurt Lewin, whose research identified three main leadership styles (Billig, 2014):

- ***Autocratic*** – the leader makes decisions without taking into account the opinions and vision of the situation of subordinates, a strict system of subordination, strict control over the execution of tasks, and minimal attention to the human factor.
- ***Democratic*** – it's about the participation of subordinates in decision-making, granting them independence by their qualifications and functions performed, supporting initiatives, and, most importantly, creating an atmosphere of trust in the organisation, which fosters a culture of growth and development.
- ***Laissez-faire*** – it's about the leader's lack of desire to take responsibility for setting goals, making decisions, motivating employees, etc.

The democratic style, built on respect, recognition of merits, and support of employees, which was characteristic of Paul Janssen, Charles Walgreen, John C. Martin, and other leaders in the pharmaceutical industry, belongs to the leadership style. It is worth noting that elements of the authoritarian leadership style can also be appropriate, but only for employees with a low level of professionalism and motivation, as well as in force majeure situations that require making quick and sole management decisions.

In behavioural theories of leadership, where the emphasis is on two dimensions, task orientation and relationship orientation, one can distinguish four leadership styles proposed by University of Michigan professor Likert (1961, 1967):

- ***Exploitative-authoritative*** – the leader alone makes decisions, evaluates information, fully controls all processes, and does not focus on subordinates.

DOI: 10.4324/9781003617266-5

- ***Benevolent-authoritative*** – the leader partially shares ideas and encourages employees, allowing them to make decisions on specific issues.
- ***Consultative*** – the leader trusts employees in many ways, uses their ideas and encourages them for their achievements, and is attentive to their needs.
- ***Participative*** – the leader trusts employees, engages them in setting goals, evaluates work, and promotes effective communication.

A participative leadership style is the most effective and efficient way for a leader to build a solid and motivated team and sustain the development of an organisation.

According to the situational theory of leadership by Hersey and Blanchard (Hersey & Blanchard, 1996; Blanchard et al., 2013), four leadership styles depend on the level of competence and commitment of employees: directing, coaching, supporting, and delegating (see Figure 4.1).

The leaders' job is to surround themself with motivated and competent people who can use the ***delegating*** leadership style. Such employees need to be given an inspiring and ambitious goal and provided with the necessary resources.

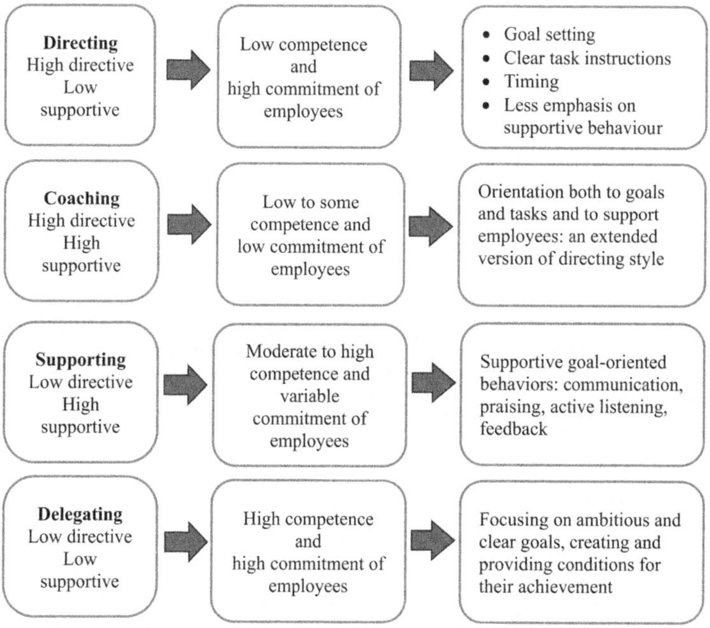


*Figure 4.1* Characteristics of leadership styles of P. Hersey and K. Blanchard.

At the same time, even the most professional and motivated employees may experience a sense of self-doubt, fear of the unknown, and be demotivated by various factors. In this case, the leader should use a ***supporting*** leadership style, which means social intelligence skills, notably emotional support. This skill is crucial as it gives employees a sense of security and confidence, fostering a positive work environment.

The 4th Industrial Revolution, AI, ML, automation, and other types of innovation, including industry-specific ones, have significantly influenced the development of modern organisations. As Klaus Schwab (2016, p. 8), founder and Executive Chairman of the World Economic Forum, noted: 'The changes are so profound that, from the perspective of human history, there has never been a time of greater promise or potential peril'. A business leader must not only consider these trends, be innovative, and have the intelligence to change but also create an atmosphere that promotes employee development and training. A ***coaching*** style of leadership allows leaders to effectively influence people in a company, especially during organisational change. This approach helps employees acquire new knowledge and skills and overcome psychological discomfort and uncertainty.

The ***directing*** leadership style is mainly used for new employees who need more competence to perform tasks and need guidance to act. Such employees are motivated to gain new knowledge and skills, so the task-oriented leadership style suits them. As a rule, business leaders surround themself with professionals with excellent competencies, so the directive leadership style is more suitable for managers.

**Food for thought:** ***Which leadership style is more effective: task-oriented or relationship-oriented?***

**How it works in the pharmaceutical industry:** Description of Paul Janssen's leadership styles according to the situational theory of leadership by Hersey and Blanchard (Lewi & Smith, 2007) (Appendix A).

## Directing

Paul Janssen's leadership style in the laboratory was marked by fairness. He selected people based on their competencies, which made using a directive leadership style unjustified and ineffective. However, he also recognised the different roles in the laboratory, distinguishing between technical staff and research scientists. This fairness in his leadership reassured the team and contributed to a positive work environment.

## Coaching

Paul Janssen paid great attention to the development of employees, the creation of innovative drugs, and the acquisition of new knowledge and skills. When Paul Janssen analysed professional scientific publications, he noted the names of employees and page numbers of articles in their area of interest on the cover, always with a note 'for discussion'. The laboratory also formed an internal information bulletin that was distributed among scientists. However, what truly set Paul Janssen apart was his personal availability to his employees. Despite his busy work schedule, he was always there for his team, ready to provide advice, support, and motivation.

## Supporting

Research involving the synthesis of new chemical compounds is often associated with difficulties, the need to find alternative options, temporary failures, and delays. Even the most competent researchers can face uncertainty, fear of failure, and other negative emotions. Paul Janssen, who was well aware of the peculiarities of conducting scientific research, tried to motivate and encourage employees to use the 'continuous critical questioning' principle. He expected professionalism, courage, and persistence from his employees. Dr Paul demonstrated these traits through his behaviour, inspiring young and more experienced employees.

## Delegating

This leadership style was the most desirable for Paul Janssen since highly motivated and professional people usually make the most brilliant scientific discoveries. Paul Janssen saw his role as creating the appropriate working conditions for them, such as a supportive and collaborative work environment, and providing them with the necessary resources, including state-of-the-art equipment and access to the latest research. For example, he did this for new employees who had previously worked in a Belgian African colony and dreamed of creating effective antiparasitic and antifungal drugs. This led to the emergence of blockbusters in the pharmaceutical market (Lewi, n.d.). In Paul Janssen's lab, formal meetings and conferences were held only in cases of lack of consensus between him and the scientists, which rarely happened. This allowed the employees to focus on their research.

## 4.2 Teams' characteristics and factors of their effectiveness

The importance of a team is challenging to overestimate since the achievement of the leader's goals and vision, as well as the sustainable development of the organisation, occurs, first of all, thanks to coordinated and effective teamwork. This increases organisational productivity, improves management decision-making quality, introduces innovations, uses organisational resources and capabilities more effectively, etc. (Parker, 1990).

A ***team*** is a group of people who are interconnected and coordinated to achieve a goal and also share common organisational values. In constructing this definition, the following elements should be noted:

- A shared goal that consolidates and directs the team's efforts, making them focused and unified in their formation.
- A group of people who work together; their effective interaction is vital in achieving a common goal. It's not just about relevant professional knowledge and skills but also the integration of views, beliefs, and worldviews.
- Shared values that are not just guidelines but the standards of behaviour that guide and align team members towards achieving a common goal.

Organisations have different types of teams (Devine et al., 1999; Ilgen, 1999; Indeed Editorial Team, 2023; Decenzo & Robbins, 2004). Thus, ***functional*** teams are characterised by employees constantly working together to solve current and interdependent problems. For example, the team of researchers in Paul Janssen's laboratory consisted of various specialists: chemists, clinicians, pharmacologists, toxicologists, statisticians, etc. Dr Paul coordinated their joint activities to achieve a common goal – creating innovative drugs.

***Cross-functional*** teams are formed from employees from different fields of activity but at the same hierarchical level. This team includes a team of product managers, in which employees from various departments interact: R&D, manufacturing, marketing, sales, etc. It was under Vasella's leadership that the activities of specialists from different functional departments of the pharmaceutical company Sandoz Pharma were united to launch the innovative anti-tumour drug Sandostatin to market (Encyclopedia.com, n.d.).

A separate group can be the ***leader's team,*** the team of key managers with whom the leader works to implement the vision and strategy for the organisation's development. For the leaders not to interfere in resolving operational issues, they must be confident in their professionalism, motivation, and commitment to the organisational values of the team members. US President Ronald Reagan noted: 'Surround yourself with the best people you can find, delegate authority, and don't interfere as long as the policy you've decided upon is being carried out' (Clifford Chance, 2019). Charles Walgreen III relied on a strong and professional management team before deciding on radical changes in the company. Having defined the vision and strategy for the company's development, he then delegated the solution of operational issues to his team.

The COVID-19 pandemic has significantly accelerated the development of digital technologies, including the format of interaction between team members. ***Virtual teams***, employees who work in different physical locations with the help of IT to achieve a common goal, have become a familiar and widespread phenomenon in organisations. Such teams have several advantages, namely flexibility and adaptability, the ability to attract talent from different parts of the world, creativity, and workplace safety. At the same time, the entire functioning of a virtual team requires a high level of trust, personal responsibility, and digital competence of the leader and the team (Lopez, 2020). One of Albert Bourla's first steps since his appointment as CEO of Pfizer in 2019 was creating a new position – CDO. This marked the beginning of the company's digital transformation in developing drugs, interacting with external stakeholders, and organising internal functional processes (Cardoso, 2021).

Several factors influence team effectiveness: clear and elevating goals, competent team members, collaborative climate, standards of excellence, external support, and recognition (Larson & LaFasto, 1989).

***A clear and elevating goal*** not only helps to achieve the desired result but also reveals the inner potential and talents of team members, focuses and directs their joint efforts, and motivates and charges them with positive energy. With a clear, inspiring, and ambitious, but at the same time achievable goal, the team will be able to implement the leader's vision and ideas.

Having a ***competent team member*** determines the effectiveness of achieving the goal. The team should consist of professional and motivated people with developed interpersonal skills who share common organisational values.

A ***collaborative climate*** is vital to effective teamwork and the ability to adapt to challenges and uncertainty. The ability to listen, accept another point of view, express your opinion without fear, and jointly seek solutions to problems contributes to creating an atmosphere of mutual trust, openness, and respect for each other.

Setting ***standards of excellence*** allows leaders to achieve ambitious goals and promotes the organisation's sustainable development. Creating and maintaining an appropriate organisational culture is necessary for team members to adhere to standards of excellence when performing tasks. The best motivator is the behaviour of a leader who not only declares the need to follow the standards of excellence but also shows their commitment to these values by their example.

***External support and recognition*** imply the availability of resources and information systems, the ability to acquire new knowledge and skills in implementing tasks, and recognition of team members' merits for achieving organisational results. The leader provides the necessary support to achieve goals, focusing on the reward system for achieving team results.

**Food for thought:** ***Can a team be effective without the leader's intervention?***

**How it works in the pharmaceutical industry:** Description of the factors influencing team effectiveness under the leadership of Filya Zhebrovska (Appendix F).

### Clear and elevating goal

Filya Zhebrovska set a clear goal for her team at Farmak: to transform the company into a modern, competitive pharmaceutical enterprise adhering to the highest international standards. The first step in this transformation was a strategic shift from producing API to manufacturing finished pharmaceutical products. By 2010, Farmak had become a leading player in Ukraine's pharmaceutical sector and began its expansion into international markets. As Filya Zhebrovska stated, 'The most important thing is to have a team of like-minded individuals with whom you can achieve the impossible. In such cases, trust becomes the driving force behind your actions' (NV, 2021).

### Competent team member

Zhebrovska assembled a team of highly skilled and motivated professionals, recognising that the success of Farmak relies on the expertise of its employees. She prioritised continuous professional development to ensure the effective implementation of innovations, including certification programs and international collaborations. Farmak has established its own training and retraining school, attended by approximately 80% of its personnel (NV, 2021). Zhebrovska ensured that her team comprised individuals with diverse competencies, including scientific research, quality control, production, and business strategy. She actively encouraged cross-functional collaboration and the adoption of methodologies, such as the Toyota Production System and Lean, to enhance efficiency and innovation across the organisation (Feshchenko, 2024).

### Collaborative climate

Zhebrovska fostered a collaborative environment at Farmak, emphasising trust and open communication. She strongly advocates building relationships within her team, consistently highlighting that a leader must unite skilled and motivated professionals. Her approach to collaboration involved engaging employees in decision-making processes and encouraging the exchange of ideas to address challenges collectively. Zhebrovska emphasises, 'A strong, united team is the main asset of any business' (Forbes, 2023). The core principles of Farmak are dedication to one's work, humanity, professionalism, and a commitment to continuous learning (NV, 2021).

### Standards of excellence

Filya Zhebrovska's commitment to excellence is one of the cornerstones of her leadership. Under her guidance, Farmak implemented rigorous quality control systems, aligning its operations with GMP standards and ensuring its products meet the highest global benchmarks. All of Farmak's production lines hold European certification, and the company's business processes are conducted according to leading international practices. These initiatives have enabled Farmak to expand its presence to over 60 global markets, including countries within the European Union (PB News, 2024).

### External support and recognition

Zhebrovska consistently ensured that her employees felt valued and supported, which played a vital role in the effectiveness of her team. She recognised the importance of providing both material and non-material support, such as access to training programmes, resources for professional growth, and fostering a culture of appreciation. At Farmak, team successes were celebrated both within the company and publicly. For instance, when Farmak launched a new pharmaceutical product or achieved a significant milestone, public announcements and celebrations were held to highlight the team's collective efforts (Farmak, n.d.). In 2024, Farmak became the only Ukrainian company to receive the prestigious international HR award, Business Culture Awards 2024, in the category of Wellbeing Initiative (Farmak, 2024).

## 4.3 Interaction between leader and team

The leader's role in forming an effective team is decisive. The leader helps team members address their problems and increases their self-confidence. The leader also fosters an inspiring vision, strategy, and values and ensures high standards of task performance, necessary resources, feedback, and understanding of each role. Notably, the leader creates conditions for the disclosure of the potential of team members, empowering them and making them feel valued. The leader also plays a crucial role in fostering 'team spirit'.

According to Collins (2001, p. 18), a company can be successful if it selects the right people – 'first got the right people on the bus, the wrong people off the bus, and the right people in the right seats—and then they figured out where to drive it'. Jim Collins (2001) identifies three principles that a leader should follow when forming their team:

- ***Principle 1***: When in doubt, don't hire – keep looking.
- ***Principle 2***: When you know you need to change personnel, act immediately.
- ***Principle 3***: Put your best people on your biggest opportunities.

***The first principle*** is based on the fact that the team, being the backbone of the company, should be created from the people most needed by the company. The leader's success mainly depends on their ability and desire to attract and retain the most talented and competent employees. Drucker noted that no company can be more successful than its people (Drucker & Maciariello, 2012).

According to ***the second principle***, a mistake in selecting a team member requires a quick decision to fire or transfer them to a more suitable position. This applies especially to people who fail to cope with the tasks assigned to them and do not want to share corporate values. Drucker (Drucker & Maciariello, 2012) stated that an incompetent and weak performer who remains in his position punishes everyone else and morally corrupts the company. At the same time, if an employee does not work well in their position, this may mean they have been assigned the wrong task or are in the wrong place. It is necessary to carefully approach the fact that honest and capable employees who have not achieved the desired result are not fired but tried in other positions where they can reveal their potential and succeed. This process of retraining and reassignment presents a promising opportunity for growth and success.

***The third principle*** guides leaders to the fact that the most professional and capable employees must be directed to solving promising issues that determine the success of the company's further development strategy. Peter Drucker emphasised that the organisation must focus more on opportunities than problems (Drucker & Maciariello, 2012).

The Hill Model for Team Leadership (Northouse, 2021) describes the interaction mechanism between the leader and the team. This model has a cascade and

*Figure 4.2* Interaction between leader and team according to the Hill Model for Team Leadership.

sequential nature and consists of the following elements: leadership decisions, leadership actions (internal or external), and team effectiveness (see Figure 4.2).

According to this model, the leader first assesses the current situation in the organisation, obtains the necessary information, analyses it, and makes ***leadership decisions.*** For instance, the leader can continue to ***monitor internal group issues*** without taking specific corrective actions. Also, based on existing trends and drivers, they can forecast ***external group issues***, adjusting the organisation's goals and strategy. However, in the event of problems that require leadership intervention, the leader ***takes action.***

Many researchers of leadership theories paid attention to two main guidelines, the effective combination of which allows for improving teamwork: task orientation and relational orientation. Hill's team leadership theory also pays attention to ***internal leadership actions.***

***Task orientation*** involves defining the team goal; structuring it (planning, organising, defining roles, delegating authority); supporting the decision-making process (informing, monitoring, coordinating, focusing on vision and values); training and developing the skills of team members necessary to complete tasks; forming high standards of work performance.

***Relational orientation*** involves supporting the team and developing practical interpersonal communication skills in its members, focusing on co-operation within the organisation, meeting the needs of employees, conflict management, forming organisational values that are important to employees, and creating a creative and friendly climate in the team.

Leadership orientation, whether task or relational, is adaptable and responsive to situational factors and the competence and motivation of employees.

According to the Hill Model for Team Leadership, a leader, in addition to internal actions aimed at task/relational, can also undertake external ***environmental*** actions to develop the team.

***External leadership actions*** involve focusing the team on its effective interaction with the external environment and support in the process of difficulties arising. In this context, the leader helps create conditions for the fruitful interaction of team members with external stakeholders, thereby opening up the opportunity for team members to develop valuable networks and alliances. This prospect and the opportunity to take on representative functions and receive external recognition contribute to the integrated development of team members and the emergence of more and more successful leaders in the company.

Successful leadership decisions and actions contribute to team ***effectiveness***. Various factors described in Section 4.2 also influence the improvement of team effectiveness, namely clear and elevating goals, competent team members, collaborative climate, standards of excellence, external support, and recognition. According to Hill's team leadership model, team effectiveness is determined by such indicators as performance and development.

Achieving organisational goals and desired results, including creating a quality product and forming a successful and recognisable brand, demonstrates high ***performance*** in a team's work under a leader's leadership. Coherence in the work of a team, effective integration of the efforts of team members in achieving goals, and meeting the needs of the leader and members of his squad characterise team ***development.*** As Daniel Vasella noted: 'Few things are as fulfilling as seeing top people grow to the next level of leadership contribution' (Cashman, 2013).

**Food for thought: *What other team-building tips do you know?***

**How it works in the pharmaceutical industry:** Description of the Hill Model for Team Leadership using Albert Bourla's interactions with the team to create a COVID-19 vaccine as an example (Appendix D).

**Leadership decisions**

- *Taking actions: Internal & External.*
  With the onset of the COVID-19 pandemic, Albert Bourla decided to create an effective vaccine as soon as possible. Despite being told

that this plan could be implemented in 18 months, Bourla persisted – six months. For this purpose, a SWAT team of highly professional employees was created. The team members were tasked to quickly establish all internal functional processes and build fruitful relationships with external stakeholders to integrate efforts against the COVID-19 pandemic (National Journal, n.d.).

- *Monitoring: Internal & External.*
  Albert Bourla made critical decisions regarding the creation of a new vaccine, which was implemented by his team both inside and outside the company. If there were no problems, Albert Bourla monitored the current situation to prevent possible difficulties. When unforeseen challenges arose, for example, in the production or transportation of vaccines, he took action. Together, optimal solutions were found. For instance, prefabricated modules were built instead of new factories to increase manufacturing capabilities (Whipple, 2022).

## Leadership actions

- *Internal: Task & Relational.*
  Albert Bourla's leadership was characterised by a balanced combination of task- and relational-oriented approaches. He set an ambitious and inspiring goal for Pfizer employees, focusing on task structuring, risk management, and standards of excellence. However, his constant motivation and inspiration during challenging and uncertain periods were equally important in maintaining high team morale.
- *External: Environmental.*
  One of the tasks that Albert Bourla set for his team was to form mutually beneficial relationships with external stakeholders. The SWAT team convinced Albert Bourla to use the new mRNA technology and start close cooperation with BioNTech. Under Albert Bourla's leadership, his team was actively involved in implementing such a project as the Global COVID-19 Medical Service Program, aimed at involving medical workers in voluntary support of public health. The SWAT team also organised the data exchange with stakeholders for a joint search for solutions, making Pfizer's tools and capabilities available to the public. Albert Bourla constantly drew attention to the role of Pfizer employees in achieving the desired result, emphasising the importance of teamwork and collective effort (National Journal, n.d.).

**Team Effectiveness**

- *Performance.*
  The performance of the team led by Albert Bourla exceeded the wildest expectations. Albert Bourla and his team responded to the threats of the COVID-19 pandemic as effectively as possible, developing the Comirnaty vaccine with 95% confirmed efficacy and the antiviral drug Paxlovid in record time. Pfizer's sales volumes were doubled compared to the pre-COVID period and reached 100 billion USD in 2022 (Kimball, 2023). This allowed the company to significantly outpace competitors in Big Pharma, strengthening its brand and reputation.
- *Development.*
  Creating a COVID-19 vaccine has significantly increased Pfizer employee engagement, team spirit, and a sense of belonging to a successful and socially oriented organisation. People were inspired and enjoyed wearing corporate T-shirts with the slogan 'Science will win'. In 2021, a survey was conducted in which 55,000 Pfizer employees took part regarding their level of satisfaction with their work at the company. The results show that over 96% are proud to work for Pfizer (Fleischmann, 2022).

## 4.4 Conclusions

1 Leadership styles depend on the specific situation, the influence of external factors, planned goals, competencies, and motivation of employees. Influential leaders combine various behaviour styles with followers. According to the situational theory of leadership by Hersey and Blanchard, the delegating leadership style is most suitable for the most professional and motivated employees. At the same time, in times of challenges and uncertainties, the developing style is an effective leadership style focused on both the task and the relationships.

2 Business leadership is defined by the presence of a team of professional and motivated employees sharing leadership goals and values. There are different types of teams depending on the goals and objectives. For example, a cross-functional team is created to launch an innovative drug successfully. A relatively new type of team is a virtual team, the emergence of which was catalysed by the COVID-19 pandemic. Various factors, including clear and elevating goals, competent team members, collaborative climate, standards of excellence, external support, and recognition, influence the effectiveness of a team.

3 Achieving desired goals and sustainable development of the organisation depends on the harmonious and effective interaction of the leader with their team. Jim Collins emphasised the critical importance of the right people in the team, whose efforts are appropriately directed to new opportunities. One of the most illustrative and comprehensive models that describes the interaction mechanism between leader and team is the Hill Model for Team Leadership. This model consists of integrated elements such as leadership decisions, leadership actions (internal or external), and team effectiveness.

## References


Billig, M., (2014). Kurt Lewin's leadership studies and his legacy to social psychology: Is there nothing as practical as a good theory? *Journal for the Theory of Social Behaviour*, 45(4), 440–460. https://doi.org/10.1111/jtsb.12074

Blanchard, K., Zigarmi, P., & Zigarmi, D., (2013). *Leadership and the One Minute Manager: Increasing Effectiveness through Situational Leadership II*. New York, NY: William Morrow.

Cardoso, J., (2021). Without digital we wouldn't be here even today – Albert Bourla, Pfizer CEO. *Medium* [online], 15 March 2021. Available from: https://joaquimcardosodorosario.medium.com/without-digital-we-wouldnt-be-here-even-today-albert-bourla-pfizer-ceo-f6f3daf4b9f3 [Accessed 05 July 2024].

Cashman, K., (2013). A Global Leader's Perspective on CEO Leadership: Part One. *Forbes* [online], 5 June 2013. Available from: https://www.forbes.com/sites/kevincashman/2013/04/18/a-global-leaders-perspective-on-ceo-leadership-part-one-2/ [Accessed 19 December 2023].

Clifford Chance, (2019). *Senior Manager Delegation – Some wise words from a US President*. Clifford Chance [online], 13 June 2019. Available from: https://www.cliffordchance.com/insights/resources/blogs/regulatory-investigations-financial-crime-insights/2019/06/senior-manager-delegation-wise-words-from-a-us-president.html [Accessed 09 January 2024].

Collins, J., (2001). *Good to Great*. London: Random House Business Books.

Decenzo, D. A., Robbins, S. P., (2004). *Human Resource Management*. 7th edition. New York: John Wiley & Sons Inc.

Devine, D.J., Clayton, L.D., Philips, J.L., Dunford, B.B., & Melner, S.B., (1999). Teams in organizations: Prevalence, characteristics, and effectiveness. *Small Group Research*, 30(6), 678–711. https://doi.org/10.1177/104649649903000602

Drucker, P., & Maciariello, J., (2012). *The Daily Drucker: 366 Days of Insight and Motivation for Getting the Right Things Done*. Russian eds. M.: Mann, Ivanov and Ferber. New York: HarperBusiness.

Encyclopedia.com, (n.d.). *Vasella, Daniel 1953– International Directory of Business Biographies*. Encyclopedia.com [online]. Available from: https://www.encyclopedia.com/economics/news-wires-white-papers-and-books/vasella-daniel-1953 [Accessed 15 January 2024].

Farmak, (2024). Farmak won an award at the international Business Culture Awards 2024 in London. Farmak [online]. Available from: https://farmak.ua/news/farmak-zdobuv-nagorodu-u-mizhnarodnomu-konkursi-business-culture-awards-2024-u-londoni/ [Accessed 20 December 2024] [Ukrainian].

Farmak, (n.d.). Unity through internal communication: Farmak's experience. Farmak [online]. Available from: https://farmak.ua/en/publication/unity-through-internal-communication-farmaks-experience/ [Accessed 20 December 2024].

Feshchenko, Y., (2024). Filia Zhebrovska explained whether lean management methodology is used at Farmak. *MC Today* [online], 19 July 2024. Available from: https://mc.today/uk/filya-zhebrovska-rozpovila-chi-pratsyuye-u-farmak-lean-metodologiya-upravlinnya/[Accessed 15 December 2024] [Ukrainian].

Fleischmann, A., (2022). Albert Bourla. Chairman and CEO, Pfizer. *Leadership Matters* [online], 5 April 2022. Available from: https://www.leadershipmattersshow.com/episodes/albert-bourla [Accessed 15 February 2024].

Forbes, (2023). *Filya Zhebrovska: 'A strong, cohesive team is the main asset of any business*. Available from: https://forbes.ua/company/filya-zhebrovska-silna-zgurtovana-komanda-golovniy-aktiv-bud-yakogo-biznesu-28062023-14430 [Accessed 15 December 2024]. [Ukrainian].

Hersey, P., & Blanchard, K.H., (1996). Great ideas revisited: Revisiting the life-cycle theory of leadership. *Training & Development Journal*, 50(1), 42.

Ilgen, D.R., (1999). Teams embedded in organisations: Some implications. *American Psychologist*, 54(2), 129–139. https://doi.org/10.1037/0003-066X.54.2.129

Indeed Editorial Team, (2023). *A guide to the different types of teams you find at work. Indeed [online]*. Available from: https://uk.indeed.com/career-advice/career-development/types-of-teams [Accessed 10 January 2024].

Kimball, S., (2023). The Covid pandemic drives Pfizer's 2022 revenue to a record $100 billion. *CNBC* [online], 2 February 2023. Available from: https://www.cnbc.com/2023/01/31/the-covid-pandemic-drives-pfizers-2022-revenue-to-a-record-100-billion.html [Accessed 11 January 2024].

Larson, C.E., & LaFasto, F.M., (1989). *Teamwork: What Must Go Right/What Can Go Wrong*. Newbury Park, CA: SAGE.

Lewi, P.J., (n.d.). Drug design with Dr. Paul Janssen. *DataScope* [online]. Available from: https://www.datascope.be/Drug%20Design/English.pdf [Accessed 23 October 2023].

Lewi, P.J., & Smith, A., (2007). Successful pharmaceutical discovery: Paul Janssen's concept of drug research. *R&D Management*, 37(4), 355–362. https://doi.org/10.1111/j.1467-9310.2007.00481.x

Likert, R., (1961). *New Patterns of Management*. New York, NY: McGraw-Hill.

Likert, R., (1967). *The Human Organisation: Its Management and Value*. New York, NY: McGraw-Hill.

Lopez, A., (2020). What is a virtual team? Definition & examples. *Project Manager* [online], 23 July 2020. Available from: https://www.projectmanager.com/blog/what-is-a-virtual-team [Accessed 10 January 2024].

National Journal, (n.d.). Business leaders: Albert Bourla. National Journal [online]. Available from: https://go.nationaljournal.com/rs/556-YEE-969/images/BusinessLeaders_Albert_Bourla.pdf [Accessed 10 August 2024].

Northouse, P.G., (2021). *Leadership: Theory and Practice*. 9th edition. Los Angeles, CA: Sage Publications.

NV, (2021). Farmak: 95 years of pharmaceutical production in Ukraine – Filia Zhebrovska. NV Ukraine [online]. Available from: https://nv.ua/ukr/ukraine/events/farmak-95-rokiv-istoriji-virobnictva-likiv-v-ukrajini-filya-zhebrovska-novini-ukrajini-50132765.html [Accessed 10 December 2024] [Ukrainian].

Parker, G.M., (1990). *Team Players and Teamwork*. San Francisco, CA: Jossey-Bass.

PB News, (2024). Forbes interviewed the chair of the supervisory board of 'Farmak', Filya Zhebrovska. *PB News* [online]. Available from: https://pb-news.info/2024/07/11/forbes-vzyav-intervyu-u-golovy-naglyadovoyi-rady-farmak-fili-zhebrovskoyi/ [Accessed 15 December 2024] [Ukrainian].

Schwab, K., (2016). The Fourth Industrial Revolution. *World Economic Forum* [online]. Available from: https://www.weforum.org/about/the-fourth-industrial-revolution-by-klaus-schwab/ [Accessed 12 January 2024].

Whipple, T., (2022). Billions at stake, endless waiting, an angry Trump: The Pfizer's CEO great vax hunt. *The Sydney Morning Herald* [online], 9 April 2022. Available from: https://www.smh.com.au/national/billions-at-stake-endless-waiting-an-angry-trump-the-pfizer-ceo-s-great-vax-hunt-20220304-p5a1q7.html [Accessed 25 February 2024].

# 5 Leadership and motivation in the pharmaceutical industry

## 5.1 The role of motivation in organisations

Motivation is the process of inducing oneself or others to take specific actions. Thus, Slocum and Hellriegel (2007) noted that motivation represents the forces acting within a person that make them behave in a specific, goal-directed manner. The definition of motivation proposed by Robbins and DeCenzo (2004) additionally characterises these forces, which are based on the needs of employees and the desire to satisfy them – the willingness to exert high levels of effort to achieve organisational goals, conditioned by the effort's ability to satisfy some individual needs.

Motivation is rooted in needs – feelings of a lack of something. Unmet needs drive the desire for specific actions to achieve the desired goal. This desire to fulfil needs shapes people's motives and conscious internal inducements based on their values and beliefs. The classical content theories of motivation, including Maslow's, Alderfer's, McClelland's, and Herzberg's, all explain the basic needs that underlie motives. This section will focus on higher needs, a characteristic often associated with leadership (see Figure 5.1).

Thus, in ***Abraham Maslow's theory***, along with basic needs, higher needs are also described: esteem and self-actualisation (Maslow, 1954). Maslow's understanding of esteem needs is multifaceted. It involves a person's desire to

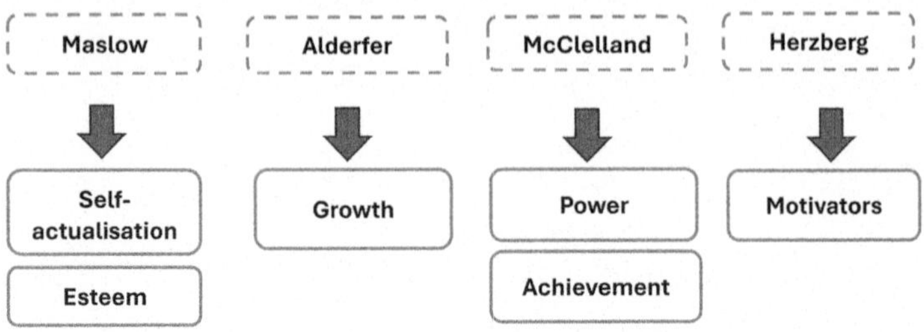


*Figure 5.1* Higher needs, according to content theories of motivation.

DOI: 10.4324/9781003617266-6

achieve goals and derive satisfaction from their accomplishments, as well as their yearning for recognition of their worth, status, and respect from others. By the need for self-actualisation, Maslow (1954, p. 46) meant 'man's desire for self-fulfilment, namely, to the tendency for him to become actualised in what he is potentially'.

According to ***Clayton Alderfer's theory*** (Alderfer, 1972), higher needs include growth needs, which imply self-esteem and self-actualisation, which are achieved through a person's achievements and talent development. Those driven by these needs strive to gain new knowledge and skills and, as a result, achieve their goals. Alderfer also noted that this need implies not only personal growth and development but also the disclosure of other people's potential. Growth needs are characteristic of leaders who satisfy these needs by forming and implementing a motivating vision for the organisation's development.

***David McClelland's theory*** highlights high-level needs, including the need for power and the need for achievement (McClelland, 1961, 1985). Those with a need for power are driven to dominate, control situations, and influence others. According to McClelland, the need for achievement is a long-term motivator for achieving goals. For success-driven individuals, the value of external rewards is secondary to the satisfaction of reaching a goal and obtaining the desired result. It's important for leaders to form teams with individuals who share this long-term commitment to success.

According to ***Frederick Herzberg's theory*** (Herzberg, 2003), two distinct groups of factors influence the motivation of employees in an organisation. These are hygiene, the absence of which leads to job dissatisfaction, and motivational, which causes job satisfaction. Higher needs include motivational factors that contribute to long-term and effective motivation, namely, achievement, recognition, work itself, responsibility, and advancement.

***Process-based theories*** substantiate not only people's needs but also the interconnection between motives, individual behaviour, their perception of desired results, and interpretation of reality. The following process theories of motivation are distinguished: expectancy theory, equity theory, and goal-setting theory.

***Expectancy theory*** is based on the VIE theory (valence, instrumentality, and expectancy) proposed by Vroom (1964), where valence is the significance of the reward (how valuable and adequate will be the reward for the result and the efforts made); instrumentality is the belief that the results obtained will lead to a reward; and expectancy is the probability that the efforts made will lead to the desired result. According to Vroom's theory, an employee will be motivated if there is an acceptable connection between the efforts made and the results, and the result obtained is perceived as an effective means of satisfying the need.

According to the ***equity theory*** by Adams (1963), people are motivated according to their perception of fairness compared to other employees. If an employee believes that they are treated worse than others, that their contribution to the organisation's development is underestimated, and that they are less trusted to participate in management decisions, then this demotivates him. As a rule, an employee subjectively compares themself with a person or group of people they perceive as a reference, occupying the same position as them in the organisation. The organisation's leader must create equal and fair conditions for all employees to increase their satisfaction, involvement, and productivity.

***The goal-setting theory*** developed by Locke and Latham (1990) highlights that goals are the most critical factors influencing employee motivation and behaviour. There are four components of the impact of goals on employees achieving the desired result:

- Purposeful coordination of the efforts of employees
- 'Charging' people with energy and enthusiasm
- Potentiation in employees of willpower and perseverance
- The opportunity to use existing skills in practice and acquire new ones

Locke and Latham (1990) identify the five main principles of setting practical goals: clarity, challenge, commitment, feedback, and task complexity. The authors note that when achieving the desired goals, standards and requirements should be further increased to solve complex problems facing challenges and uncertainties.

In addition to the motivation theories discussed, the ***self-determination theory***, proposed by Ryan and Deci (2000), is worth highlighting. This model illustrates the continuum of intrinsic and extrinsic motivational factors. Extrinsic motivation includes controlled motivation, which implies the desire to avoid punishment or obtain incentive, and autonomous motivation, which consists of the employee's willingness to be helpful and involved in organisational activities by accepted organisational values and behaviour patterns. In turn, intrinsic motivation is the employee's desire to achieve goals, which brings interest, pleasure from the process, and the opportunity to satisfy various needs.

It is worth noting that such leadership theories as Bass's transformational theory and Heifitz's adaptive theory focus on creating conditions for motivating personnel to achieve organisational goals through the leader's example, the ability to inspire and instil confidence in people even in the most challenging and uncertain situations.

**Food for thought:** ***Which theory of motivation is most closely related to leadership?***

**How it works in the pharmaceutical industry:** Description of goal-setting theory using Charles Walgreen III's motivation of his team as an example (Collins, 2001) (Appendix C).

### Clarity

Upon Charles Walgreen III's appointment as CEO of Walgreens in 1971, a new vision for the company's growth was unveiled – to become the most convenient pharmacy with the highest profitability per customer visit. A customer-centric organisational culture, a pioneering concept at the time, supported this vision. According to the vision, clear and achievable goals were formed to transform Walgreens into the leading pharmacy chain in the United States.

### Challenge

The implementation of Walgreens' new vision implied setting ambitious and motivating goals. To achieve these goals, it was necessary to quickly and effectively implement service, technology, and business-process innovations. As a result, Walgreens, in the early 1980s, became a pioneer in creating the Intercom electronic network, allowing customer information accumulation in one information centre. The company also became the first in the pharmacy market to use a computerised inventory control system, scanners, etc.

### Commitment

To commit to Walgreens' new vision and organisational goals, Charles Walgreen III built a dedicated and motivated management team around him who shared his values and aspirations. Through effective collaboration with his team, Walgreens' stock price has surpassed the market average several times.

### Feedback

Charles 'Cork' Walgreen III, despite his outward calm, was determined and never retreated or doubted. The example of selling restaurants over five years demonstrated his attitude and strong character. His clear feedback consistently guided his team – implementing the vision and goals should proceed as planned. At the same time, Charles Walgreen III tried not to interfere in operational processes, giving the necessary powers to the company's managers.

### Task complexity

Successfully implementing Walgreens' vision required setting comprehensive goals to improve the company's customer focus. For example, the decision was made to open pharmacies at street corners (corner pharmacies) and track each pharmacy's profitability per customer visit. This approach contributed to the increase in convenient services for visitors, such as 'photo in an hour'.

## 5.2 Characteristics of extrinsic motivational factors

The practical and long-term motivation of personnel in an organisation depends on the integrated use of external and internal motivational factors. For example, Herzberg (2003) noted the importance of hygiene factors, namely, work conditions, company policy and administration, salary, supervision, relationships with peers, etc., the absence or insufficient level of which leads to employee dissatisfaction and decreased motivation.

According to transformational leadership theory, employee performance can exceed expectations with an effective combination of transactional and transformational leadership. The transactional approach implies a mutually beneficial exchange between the leader and employees of the organisation, for example, the desired level of financial reward in exchange for effectively completed work (Bass, 1990; Bass & Avolio, 1994).

Based on various theories of motivation and leadership, such clusters of external motivation as negative motivators, financial and relatively financial positive motivators, and non-financial positive motivators can be distinguished (Aliekperova, 2018) (see Table 5.1).

***Negative motivators***, which Herzberg (2003) described as 'pushing' but not motivating factors, are not leadership tools for interacting with employees. However, they can be used in accordance with internal organisational regulations and rules.

***Financial motivators***, which include cash bonuses and benefits packages, help to meet various needs. For example, according to Maslow (1954), financial rewards help to increase social status and invest in personal development and self-realisation. At the same time, many scientists questioned the effectiveness of financial rewards for an organisation's successful and sustainable development. Thus, Herzberg (2003) noted that monetary rewards

*Table 5.1* Classification of external motivation factors

| *Negative* | *Positive* | |
|---|---|---|
| | *Financial and relatively financial* | *Non-financial* |
| • Disciplinary action<br>• Use of penalty scheme<br>• Cancelling cash bonuses or diminishing their extent | • Cash bonuses<br>• Benefits package (medical insurance, mobile communication compensation, automobile, etc.).<br>• Promotion possibilities | • Recognition<br>• Participation in making organisational decisions<br>• Feedback<br>• Clear organisational goals<br>• Creation and support of a friendly corporate climate<br>• Maintaining a work-life balance |

only contribute to short-term motivation. Kohn (1993) argued that there is no scientifically proven evidence that introducing a financial reward system could improve personnel's long-term performance and quality. He noted that the emphasis on using financial rewards as the primary motivator can destroy internal motivation. Deming viewed monetary rewards as a straightforward approach often used by managers who do not fully understand how to manage internal motivation (Neave, 1990).

***Promotion possibilities*** can be attributed to relatively financial motivators, as they are associated with the possibility of increasing financial rewards. Career growth is a powerful motivator for individuals with a significant need for power, as per McClelland (1961, 1985), for whom it is essential to influence others and have enough authority. Similarly, those with a strong need for achievement see career growth as a way to achieve their goals more effectively.

In managing a team, a leader must employ a balanced mix of ***financial and non-financial motivators***, recognising the complexity of human motivation.

***Recognition*** is one of the most important non-financial motivators in an organisation, as it allows employees to understand that their efforts, behaviour, and achievements are valued and essential to the organisation. This non-financial reward tool helps to satisfy the need for respect, which, according to Maslow (1954), can be assessed as the desire for achievement, positive reputation, and status. Other forms of recognition include trust from management and colleagues, providing a greater degree of responsibility, the opportunity to participate in interesting and ambitious projects, etc.

***Participation in making organisational decisions*** allows employees to feel like full-fledged team members and realise their contribution to the organisation's success. If employees in the organisation cannot fully participate in the decision-making process, this worsens the organisational climate, contributes to the outflow of professionals, and, as a result, negatively affects the successful and sustainable development of the organisation.

***Feedback***, as a non-financial motivator, is crucial in helping employees evaluate their professional activities and improve their competencies. For instance, for employees with less experience, feedback is a tool for enhancing their professional skills, setting work priorities, and boosting their confidence and motivation. It's equally essential for experienced employees to share their competencies and participate in decision-making to enhance their motivation and engagement.

The importance of ***clear organisational goals*** is described in detail in Locke and Latham's Goal Setting Theory (Locke & Latham, 1990). Furthermore, an inspiring vision, mission, and structured strategy for the organisation's development, along with clear organisational goals, not only meets the various needs of employees but also serves as a driving force for business success. It is worth noting that all successful leaders in the pharmaceutical industry formed a vision and mission that inspired employees to achieve the desired result.

***Creation and support of a friendly corporate climate*** largely depend on the organisational culture, the absence of prerequisites for conflicts based on an unfair reward system, irrational distribution of resources, and other factors that reduce motivation. The company's leader influences the formation of organisational values, creating a favourable and motivating internal environment to achieve the desired results. According to research by Kessler and Purcell (1992), all successful companies have formed stable, inspiring organisational values. A clear relationship was found between the positive attitude of employees to organisational values and the level of motivation and satisfaction of employees.

***Maintaining a work-life balance*** allows employees to integrate work functions with their personal lives effectively. This balance is expressed in the creation of convenient work schedules, the ability to regulate the length of the working day, and a more flexible organisation of work. The COVID-19 pandemic has necessitated significant adjustments to the work process, making hybrid or remote work a familiar format for employees. Despite the need to improve digital literacy, the ability to fully utilise remote work tools such as Zoom, Microsoft Teams, Google Meet, etc. and hybrid or remote work provides mutual benefits for employers and employees. According to Half (2023), nine out of ten employees are considering hybrid or remote work opportunities. Currently, pharmaceutical companies are actively using this format, including creating conditions for the functioning of virtual teams.

**Food for thought: *Why is extrinsic motivation insufficient to achieve long-term goals?***

**How it works in the pharmaceutical industry:** Description of external motivators using the example of Daniel Vasella's interaction with Novartis employees (Appendix E).

### Negative motivators

According to the Novartis (2018) Code of Conduct, disciplinary standards may be applied to employees, including possible termination, if they violate the company's norms and rules of conduct. It is worth noting that ***negative motivators*** are managerial, not leadership tools.

### Positive financial and relatively financial motivators

Daniel Vasella established a programme of financial rewards for employees based on their performance, which was paid partly in cash and partly in options (Encyclopedia.com, n.d.). He created a venture fund of 80 million dollars to help former employees of Novartis develop start-ups. In addition to financial motivators like ***cash bonuses and benefits packages***, the leader of Novartis motivated his employees through relatively financial motivators. Thus, the top management development programme in Novartis, initiated by Vasella, provided additional ***promotion possibilities*** for employees (Betov & Szillat, 2016).

### Positive non-financial motivators

To demonstrate ***recognition*** of the merits and achievements of his team members, Daniel Vasella used financial rewards, career advancement opportunities, and non-financial motivators. Vasella involved employees at different management levels ***to participate in making organisational decisions*** at Novartis. He described this approach as a 'Top Down, Bottom Up, Top Down' process, emphasising the collaborative nature of decision-making (Encyclopedia.com, n.d.). This meant that top management would identify key development goals, submit them for review and discussion, and then make decisions based on the suggestions and recommendations received through ***feedback***. Daniel Vasella recognised the importance of ***clear organisational goals*** for employee motivation. He believed that the leader's task 'is to recognise the right goal and path forward and then to align and persuade people to do the things you believe will be relevant for the long-term success of the company' (Kirkland, 2012). Daniel Vasella contributed to the ***creation and support of a friendly corporate climate***. He tried to be sincere with his employees, support them, provide them with the necessary resources, create conditions for attracting new talent to the company, and more. Daniel Vasella emphasised the importance of maintaining physical and mental health for long-term leadership and goal achievement. He also created conditions for ***maintaining a work-life balance*** for his employees.

## 5.3 Characteristics of intrinsic motivational factors

According to Herzberg (2003), motivational factors that focus on intrinsic motivation bring job satisfaction. Ryan and Deci (2000), the authors of the self-determination theory of motivation, emphasised the importance of intrinsic motivation, as it ensures happiness, interest, pleasure, and joy. A successful leader competently and for the organisation's benefit uses people's internal motives and aspirations, their desire to achieve results, be proud of their work, benefit society, etc. Drucker noted that the task of top management is to improve the company's performance, using the strengths and healthy desire for the success of individuals (Drucker & Maciariello, 2012).

The following types of intrinsic motivation can be distinguished (Aliekperova, 2018):

- Achievement of organisational goals
- Interesting and motivating work
- Feeling of pride in one's work
- A leader's personality and ability to inspire
- Opportunity to obtain new knowledge and skills

***The achievement of organisational goals*** can be a strong motivator as it satisfies a person's need for respect, growth, and self-actualisation. Success in itself can be a motivating factor, especially for individuals who have a need for achievement, according to McClelland's theory.

***Interesting and motivating work*** is a powerful intrinsic motivator, as it helps employees get joy and pleasure from their tasks. Peter Drucker noted that employees of successful companies enjoy their work (Drucker & Maciariello, 2012), and Herzberg (2003, p. 1) wrote the following: 'Forget praise. Forget punishment. Forget cash. You need to make their jobs more interesting'.

***A feeling of pride in one's work*** is an essential factor of internal motivation, directly related to the work's content and achieving the desired result. The company's leader needs to form a system of values in the organisation that allows employees to be proud of their work. These values should be socially significant and focused on compliance with moral and ethical principles. Employees' involvement and personal contribution to the process of successful goal achievement allow them to feel pride in their work. In his lectures, Deming emphasised that only pride in one's work brings joy (Neave, 1990).

***A leader's personality and ability to inspire*** can be considered an intrinsic motivator if the leader is a role model. Leaders who inspire followers by example are competent professionals who can effectively interact with people and have a clear and understandable vision for the organisation's development. Transformational, adaptive, authentic, and servant leaders are also examples of leaders who have the ability to inspire their followers.

***The opportunity to obtain new knowledge and skills*** is an intrinsic motivator for employees with a developed need for growth and self-development. Drucker (1999) noted that knowledge ceases to be an abstract value and becomes a resource that brings practical benefits. A leader's crucial role is to create conditions that encourage and empower employees to strive for self-education and use new competencies to achieve goals. Deming noted the importance of obtaining knowledge in his lectures at New York University, saying that an organisation does not just need good employees – it needs people who improve themselves through education (Neave, 1990).

**Food for thought:** ***What is the difference between inspiration and motivation?***

**How it works in the pharmaceutical industry:** Description of intrinsic motivators using the example of Paul Janssen's interaction with his team (Lewi & Smith, 2007) (Appendix A).

## Achievement of organisational goals

Paul Janssen formed a team of highly motivated professionals who worked enthusiastically to create new medicines. The primary motivator for researchers was to create patentable inventions that would help people cope with various diseases and symptoms and have commercial success.

**Interesting and motivating work**

Working in the laboratory was a favourite pastime for Janssen and his team, to which they devoted much time and energy. They received internal satisfaction from creating new drugs, the opportunity to professionally interact with colleagues, participating in scientific and practical conferences, publishing scientific articles, etc.

**A feeling of pride in one's work**

Involving in creating innovative drugs gave Paul Janssen's team of researchers a sense of pride. The opportunity to work in one of the most successful laboratories with outstanding and talented people also contributed to the formation of internal motivation among the employees, who felt pride not only for their achievements but also for their team's achievements.

**Leader's personality and ability to inspire**

Paul Janssen was a role model and inspirational leader for generations of scientists and researchers. Dr Paul's personality inspired his staff and scientists worldwide, such as John C. Martin. In memory of this legendary figure, the Dr Paul Janssen Award for Biomedical Research has been awarded annually since 2004 to scientists who have significantly improved human health (Johnson & Johnson, n.d.).

**Opportunity to obtain new knowledge and skills**

Dr Paul valued not only his employees' professionalism but also their curiosity, courage, creativity, adaptability, and ability to think critically. Paul Janssen created conditions for the intellectual stimulation of his employees, for developing their scientific potential and acquiring additional knowledge and skills.

## 5.4 Conclusions

1 Achieving organisational goals depends on the leader's ability to effectively inspire employees, understand their needs and motives, and create conditions for the formation of people's internal desire to achieve the desired result. Content theories of motivation emphasise higher needs, including the need for respect, self-actualisation, achievement, etc. According to

process-based theories, compelling staff motivation depends on inspiring goals, satisfaction with the results achieved, a fair reward system, etc.

2 Based on the mutually beneficial interaction between the leader and followers, external motivation can be considered from the position of the following clusters: negative motivators, financial and relatively financial positive motivators, and non-financial positive motivators. Internal organisational regulations and rules regulate the use of negative motivators. Using financial and relatively financial positive motivators is based on the transactional approach to leadership. However, excessive concentration on these factors can negatively affect internal motivation. Non-financial positive motivators improve the relationship between the leader and employees and inspire them to achieve goals.

3 Creating conditions for forming employees' internal motivation is a leader's essential task, as its impact is the most enduring in achieving goals. For instance, when employees feel involved in developing innovative and effective medication therapy based on high standards for maintaining health and improving people's quality of life, it has a powerful and inspiring effect on them. A business leader's ability to effectively blend external and internal motivation factors is essential for the organisation's sustainable development.

## References


Adams, J.S., (1963). Toward an understanding of inequity. *Journal of Abnormal and Social Psychology*, 67, 422–436.

Alderfer, C.P., (1972). *Existence, Relatedness and Growth: Human Needs in Organisational Setting*. New York: Free Press.

Aliekperova, N., (2018). Motivating factors effecting work efficiency of employees in Ukrainian pharmaceutical sector. *Economics and Sociology*, 11(1), 61–74. doi: 10.14254/2071-789X.2018/11-1/4

Bass, B.M., (1990). From transactional to transformational leadership: Learning to share the vision. *Organisational Dynamics*, 18, 19–31. https://doi.org/10.1016/0090-2616(90)90061-S

Bass, B.M., & Avolio, B.J., (1994). *Improving Organisational Effectiveness through Transformational Leadership*. Thousand Oaks, CA: Sage.

Betov, A., & Szillat, P., (2016). Business leadership concepts exemplified by the two exceptional leaders Daniel Vasella and Ricardo Semler. *Journal of Contemporary Economic and Business Issues*, 3(1), 32–60.

Collins, J., (2001). *Good to Great*. London: Random House Business Books.

Drucker, P., (1999). *Management Challenges for the 21st Century*. New York: HarperCollins.

Drucker, P., & Maciariello, J., (2012). *The Daily Drucker: 366 Days of Insight and Motivation for Getting the Right Things Done*. Russian eds. M.: Mann, Ivanov and Ferber. New York: Harper Collins.

Encyclopedia.com, (n.d.). Vasella, Daniel 1953 – International Directory of Business Biographies. *Encyclopedia.com* [online]. Available from: https://www.encyclopedia.com/economics/news-wires-white-papers-and-books/vasella-daniel-1953 [Accessed 15 January 2024].

Half, R., (2023). The State of Remote Work: 5 Trends to Know for 2023. *PR Newswire* [online], 21 February 2023. Available from: https://www.prnewswire.com/news-releases/the-state-of-remote-work-5-trends-to-know-for-2023-301751351.html [Accessed 12 January 2024].

Herzberg, F., (2003). One more time: How do you motivate employees. *Harvard Business Review*, 81, 86–96.

Johnson & Johnson, (n.d.). *Dr Paul Janssen Award* [online]. Johnson & Johnson. Available from: https://www.pauljanssenaward.com/ [Accessed 07 March 2024].

Kessler, I., & Purcell, J., (1992). Performance-related pay: Objectives and application. *Human Resource Management Journal*, 2(3), 16–33. https://doi.org/10.1111/j.1748-8583.1992.tb00258.x

Kirkland, R., (2012). Leading in the 21st century: An interview with Daniel Vasella. *McKinsey & Company* [online], 01 September 2012. Available from: https://www.mckinsey.com/featured-insights/leadership/an-interview-with-daniel-vasella [Accessed 24 December 2023].

Kohn, A., (1993). Why incentive plans cannot work. *Harvard Business Review*, September–October, pp. 54–63.

Lewi, P.J., & Smith, A., (2007). Successful pharmaceutical discovery: Paul Janssen's concept of drug research. *R&D Management*, 37(4), 355–362. https://doi.org/10.1111/j.1467-9310.2007.00481.x

Locke, A.M., & Latham, G.P., (1990). *A Theory of Goal Setting and Task Performance*. Englewood Cliffs, NY: Prentice-Hall.

Maslow, A., (1954). *Motivation and Personality*. New York: Harper & Row.

McClelland, D.C., (1985). *Human Motivation*. Glenview, IL: Scott, Foresman.

McClelland, D.C., (1961). *The Achieving Society*. Princeton, NJ: Van Nostrand Company Inc.

Neave, H.R., (1990). *The Deming Dimension*. Knoxville, TN: SPC Press.

Novartis, (2018). *Code of Conduct – Switzerland*. Basel: Novartis AG.

Raven, J., (1984). *Competence in Modern Society: Its Identification, Development and Release*. Oxford, England: Oxford Psychologists Press.

Robbins, S.P., & DeCenzo, D.A., (2004). *Fundamentals of Management: Essential Concepts and Applications*. Upper Saddle River, New Jersey: Pearson Prentice Hall.

Ryan, R.M., & Deci, E.L., (2000). Self-determination theory and the facilitation of intrinsic motivation, social development, and well-being. *The American Psychologist*, 55(1), 68–78. https://doi.org/10.1037/0003-066X.55.1.68

Slocum, J.W., & Hellriegel, D., (2007). *Fundamentals of Organizational Behavior*. Mason: South-Western/Cengage Learning.

Vroom, V., (1964). *Work and Motivation*. New York: Wiley and Sons.

# 6 Leadership ethics and innovations in the pharmaceutical industry

## 6.1 Foundations and principles of ethical leadership

The leader's behaviour, values, relationships with followers, and decision-making characteristics are considered from the point of view of ethics. According to Drucker (Klein, 2000), business and ethics are inseparable concepts. Kouzes and Posner (1987) emphasised the urgent need for the leader's actions to be based on compliance with ethical standards. Burns (2003, p. 319) noted that leaders should 'pass the test of ethics and values'.

A leader's ethics can be characterised by their behaviour or character. Leadership behaviour is viewed through the lens of ***teleology*** (what an individual focuses on when making decisions and their consequences) and ***deontology*** (what an individual should do to fulfil their moral and ethical obligations). The presence of *virtues* shapes a leader's character.

From the perspective of teleology, a leader can prioritise personal interests over the interests of others – ***ethical egoism***; strive to create the greatest good for the most significant number of people – ***utilitarianism***; or show concern for the welfare of others rather than one's interests – ***altruism***. In the context of business, ethical egoism often takes precedence. However, given the multitude of stakeholders with whom companies engage, many management decisions are guided by utilitarianism. At first glance, altruism may not seem the most fitting approach for business. Yet companies that invest resources in the community, integrate the principles of the circular economy into their organisational strategy, and demonstrate social responsibility lay the groundwork for their successful and sustainable development.

From the perspective of deontology, a leader's commitment to moral and ethical principles is paramount. Their sincerity in words and actions, generosity, and respect for others set a strong foundation for ethical leadership. In business organisations, this translates to aligning the leader's and team's behaviour with the organisation's mission and values and, crucially, fostering transparency in decision-making. This transparency, along with implementing policies, procedures, and rules, deters unethical behaviour in companies.

DOI: 10.4324/9781003617266-7

If, in teleology and deontology, the object of study is an individual's behaviour, then in theories of virtue, it is their personality. According to Aristotle, virtue and morality are not innate but are acquired by a person throughout life, emphasising the need for lifelong learning and growth (Kleinman, 2013). Many leadership theories, such as the trait approach, transformational leadership, authentic leadership, servant leadership, and inclusive leadership, are based on the theory of virtues.

According to Kohlberg (1984), ethical standards can be developed and typically progress through three successive levels:

- ***pre-conventional morality,*** based on self-interest, avoiding punishment and rewards;
- ***conventional morality,*** based on society's views and expectations; and
- ***post-conventional morality,*** based on conscience and creating a just society.

From a leadership perspective, post-conventional morality is the last level of most significant interest. This level is characterised by the desire to create a common good for all while considering the interests of different stakeholders, which is of particular importance for leadership in the pharmaceutical industry. As Burns (1978, p. 18) noted: 'Moral leadership emerges from, and always returns to, the fundamental wants and needs, aspirations, and values of the followers'. Ethical leadership is based on the following principles (Northouse, 2021):

- Respect others
- Show justice
- Manifest honesty
- Build community
- Serve others

***Respecting others*** means being attentive to the needs of other people. A leader who respects other people considers employees' professional aspirations, allows them to show creative initiative, and accepts their personal characteristics. This not only promotes a positive work environment but also boosts their employees' involvement and motivation in achieving organisational goals. Respect for another person is a mutual process that implies appropriate employee behaviour. Bower (1997) noted that in all successful professional groups, respect for the individual is determined not by position but by competence, reputation, and leadership qualities.

***Justice*** as an ethical principle of leadership is based on the leader's commitment to ensuring common rights and opportunities for all followers. This principle, as detailed by the American philosopher Rawls (1971) in his theory of justice, asserts that justice is the primary virtue of social institutions. It upholds that all individuals, irrespective of their social standing, are entitled to equal rights, freedom, and respect for their rights and interests. In organisations, this principle is manifested in resource allocation, employee remuneration, and compliance with Equity, Diversity, and Inclusion (EDI) policy. Beauchamp and Bowie (1988) emphasised the importance of individual needs, a person's rights, individual effort, societal contribution, and merit or performance, even in a system of equal rights and opportunities.

***Manifest honesty*** – this principle of ethical leadership underscores the crucial role of leaders in building and maintaining trust and loyalty among their followers. Jack Welch noted that people with integrity tell the truth, take responsibility for past actions, admit mistakes, and fix them (Welch & Welch, 2005). If a leader is not sincere in their words and actions, then over time, they lose the trust of their employees, clients, shareholders, and other stakeholders. As a result, insincerity leads to relationships ceasing to be effective and mutually beneficial.

***Building a community*** is a principle that hinges on forming a common goal by the leader, a goal that inspires their followers. From an ethical standpoint, the achievement of this goal should bring value not only to the leader but also to all participants in the process. As Burns (1978, p. 36) succinctly stated: 'I define leadership as leaders inducing followers to act for certain goals that represent the values and the motivations…of both leaders and followers'. A leader who manipulates people and focuses solely on their own well-being will not be able to build a sustainable business. It's crucial that the common goal is an inspiring factor, contributing to the resolution of significant social issues.

***Serve others*** – this ethical leadership principle is based mainly on altruistic behaviour when an individual cares more about other people's well-being than theirs. Many leadership theories are based on the 'serves others' principle: transformational leadership, authentic leadership, servant leadership, inclusive leadership, etc. Aristotle believed that performing virtuous acts leads to a special state – happiness (Kleinman, 2013). In this context, it is worth quoting the famous philosopher and humanist Albert Schweitzer: 'I don't know what your destiny will be, but one thing I know: the only ones among you who will be really happy are those who will have sought and found how to serve' (Forbes, n.d.). In the pharmaceutical industry, the principle of serving people is key since companies' main goal is to maintain people's health and quality of life.

**Food for thought:** ***What can you contribute to the existing principles of ethical leadership in the pharmaceutical industry?***

**How it works in the pharmaceutical industry:** Description of Roy Vagelos's principles of ethical leadership using the example of the MDP (Vagelos & Galambos, 2006) (Appendix F).

**Respects others**

Receiving necessary medical and pharmaceutical care is fundamental for observing human rights. The implementation of Mectizan Donation Program (MDP) has made it possible to provide healthcare to all people needing treatment for river blindness in the most inaccessible corners of the planet.

**Shows justice**

Developing, researching, producing, and launching an innovative drug is a multi-stage and expensive project. The implementation of MDP has made it possible to achieve social justice: regardless of financial capabilities, people could receive adequate treatment for river blindness.

**Manifests honesty**

The implementation of the MDP was made possible by the sincere desire of Roy Vagelos, enthusiastic scientists, and others to help people suffering from river blindness. Roy Vagelos' sincerity was demonstrated by Merk taking on the financial responsibility for distributing Mektizan drug to remote areas. This significantly contributed to the building of trust between Merk and the stakeholders.

**Builds community**

The inspiring goal of helping people suffering from river blindness united people: a committee was created to regulate the work of leading scientists worldwide, a logistics chain was built, etc. Despite the initial difficulties, Roy Vagelos was able to attract international organisations, sponsorships, etc. to this problem.

**Serves others**

MDP has become one of the longest-running and most successful programmes, saving many lives. Roy Vagelos noted, 'Our policy on Mectizan and other gifts make Merck a place where people were proud and excited to work because they wanted to make lives better around the world' (Vagelos & Galambos, 2006, p. 169).

## 6.2 Destructive and unethical leadership

The success of the pharmaceutical business relies heavily on launching innovative healthcare products. However, the pursuit of market leadership and financial success can lead to a detrimental impact. For instance, between 1999 and 2016, pharmaceutical companies in the United States paid over $33 billion to state and federal authorities for illegal activities in drug research, production, and promotion. The industry's reputation, which is worse than that of other business sectors, plays a significant role in shaping the future of biomedical research, and any negative impact can be far-reaching (Arnold et al., 2022).

Unethical behaviour in the pharmaceutical industry typically affects three key areas: R&D, competition, and promotion (Santoro & Gorrie, 2005; Green, 2008) (see Figure 6.1).

In addition to the deterioration of reputation, which may lead to a decrease in critical business indicators, unethical actions by companies in the pharmacy can have negative consequences for the health of patients. It's crucial to remember that the primary goal of the pharmaceutical business is to promote and protect patient well-being. The responsibility for maintaining an ethical organisational culture and preventing unethical and destructive behaviour lies heavily on the shoulders of the company's leader. A leader who disregards ethical and moral standards creates and maintains an organisational culture in which achieving desired financial results becomes more important than the health and lives of patients.

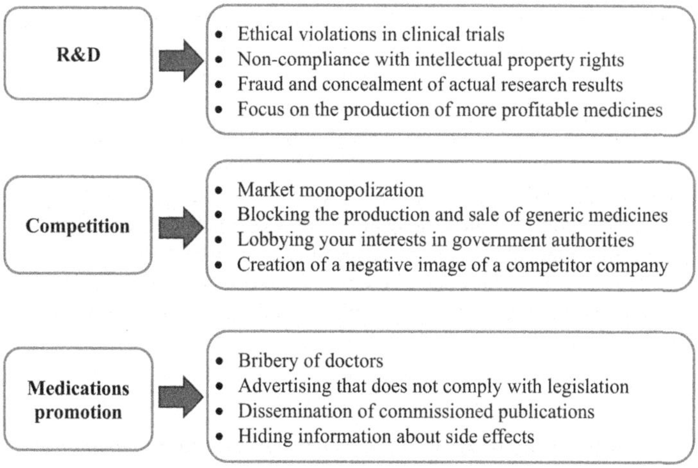


*Figure 6.1* Examples of destructive and unethical behaviour in the pharmaceutical industry.

Burns (1978) described the destructive leader type as a pseudo-transformational leader. Unlike the transformational leader, for whom ethics is of crucial importance, the pseudo-transformational leader is focused exclusively on achieving his own goals while ignoring the moral values and interests of others. Such leaders may have leadership traits such as willpower, persistence, self-confidence, the ability to convince followers, and other outstanding qualities. Still, they use them for manipulation and personal gain.

Padilla et al. (2007) proposed a 'toxic triangle' model consisting of the following components:

- Destructive leaders
- Susceptible followers
- Conducive environment

***Destructive leaders*** are characterised by the ability to influence and manipulate other people, a tendency towards narcissism, vanity, and excessive ambition. As a rule, such leaders have negative life stories that influence the formation of their immoral and destructive worldviews.

***Susceptible followers*** of a destructive leader are divided into two types: colluders and conformers.

***Colluders*** follow a destructive leader because their ambitions strive to obtain the desired status and personal gain; they also share the worldview of such a leader and his system of values, characterised by greed and selfishness.

***Conformers*** are drawn to a leader who can help them satisfy their innate need to belong to a community. They are psychologically immature, have low self-esteem, and lack moral and value guidelines. The leader's behaviour and actions serve as a norm for them, influencing their actions and decisions. This influence can lead them into the process of various destructive actions.

The presence of a ***conducive environment*** characterises destructive leadership. Uncertainty and constant anxiety allow the leader to form a sense of insecurity in their followers, which they use to implement unethical actions. The values that reflect the behaviour model of a destructive leader are aimed at suppressing mutually beneficial cooperation, independent behaviour, the desire for justice, etc. This atmosphere is characterised by intrigue, mutual accusations, closed and ineffective communications, and the formation of a 'personality cult'.

**Food for thought: *How can destructive leadership be eliminated in the pharmaceutical industry?***

**How it works in the pharmaceutical industry:** Description of destructive leadership using the example of the CEO of Ranbaxy, Malvinder Mohan Singh (Eban, 2019) (Appendix H).

**Destructive leader**

Former CEO of Ranbaxy Malvinder Singh became such a leader. Despite his brilliant education, personal charisma, self-confidence, and determination, Singh was overly ambitious. Regardless of the law and ethics, he achieved what he wanted by any means. In 2009, after several scandals, he was forced to resign from Ranbaxy's CEO post. In 2019, Malvinder Singh was arrested on fraud charges.

**Susceptible followers – Colluders**

The colluders were Ranbaxy's top management, who shared Malvinder Singh's values, particularly his brother Shivinder Singh. Managers who opposed the brothers' business practices were forced to leave the company.

**Susceptible followers – Conformers**

Numerous Ranbaxy employees were involved in Malvinder Singh and his team's misconduct. This was possible for various reasons, including fear, poverty, a lack of moral compass, and peculiarities of the local business culture.

**Conducive environment**

Ranbaxy's organisational culture was based on fraud, data concealment and falsification, and the provision of false information. In the process of such deception, clinical trial results were falsified, GMP standards were systematically violated, and false data was provided to regulatory authorities such as FDA.

## 6.3 Types of innovations

Business innovation is the driving force behind its development. According to the Oslo Manual (OECD, 2010, p. 9), 'Innovation drives growth and helps address social challenges'. Various drivers, such as environmental pressure, knowledge exchange between partners, business strategy and related innovation strategy, technological capabilities, and company capacity, determine the need for innovation (Demeter, 2023).

The pharmaceutical industry is one of the most innovative, and global pharmaceutical companies such as Novartis, Roche, Pfizer, Merck, and Johnson & Johnson invest in R&D on average for up to 20% of their revenue. The creation and development of novel drugs, a complex multi-stage process, involves about 10–15 years of experiments and optimisation, with each new drug costing about 1–2 billion dollars (Al-Madhagi, 2023). As Gambardella (1995, p. 165) rightly pointed out, 'Innovation is the single most important source of competitiveness among large pharmaceutical firms'. Companies that do not invest enough in R&D risk losing their competitive advantages and market leadership (Arnold et al., 2022). John C. Martin stated: 'We must continue to innovate to make our own products obsolete' (Lou et al., 2022).

Pharmaceutical companies' innovation policy depends on external and internal factors. The main external factors are regulatory policy and patent legislation, population morbidity trends, new technologies in the development, research, and manufacturing of drugs, competitors' positions, the life cycle of analogue medications, etc. Internal factors include the material and technical base level, the availability of the necessary resources, the presence of professional and motivated personnel, and an innovative leader. Thanks to leadership, an effective strategy for implementing innovations in the company's activities is created, an organisational culture is formed, contributing to the development of innovations, and fruitful interactions with academic and research centres are developed.

It is of utmost importance for a leader to be able to seize opportunities that arise in the market. The creation of a COVID-19 vaccine is a perfect example of this. Thanks to this, Pfizer was able to get ahead of its competitors and take a leading position in the market. As Albert Bourla noted: 'Luck never comes to the unprepared and this company was preparing for this moment' (Writer, 2021).

It is worth noting that business innovation is not only product/service or technology innovation but also business process innovation (Demeter, 2023).

***Product innovation*** in the pharmaceutical industry includes novel medications, biosimilars, medicines with newly identified properties, medicines with a modified dosage form, innovative medical devices, and other innovative healthcare products. ***Service innovation*** provides new opportunities for customers to purchase, use, and dispose of healthcare products.

The Fourth Industrial Revolution has significantly impacted ***technology innovation***. AI, ML, automation, etc. have become prerequisites for fast-moving company development. Pharmaceutical organisations use modern technologies in R&D, pharmaceutical production, distribution, logistics, marketing, and other functional processes.

***Business process innovation*** is a multifaceted concept that includes innovations in organisational architecture and management tools. These innovations directly impact the efficiency of various business processes, such as marketing and sales, CX, distribution and logistics, production, R&D, and more. In addition to technological drivers and the need for rapid adaptation to environmental factors, business process innovation is also influenced by paradigm shifts in the development of the economy and business.

The task of the leader and their team in this process is to effectively integrate different types of innovation to achieve strategic business goals. Equally important is creating an organisational culture that supports innovation. It's important to remember that while innovations are not the sole key to success, they are a necessary 'ingredient' for companies striving to take and maintain leadership positions.

**Food for thought:** ***How can a leader foster an innovative business environment in the pharmaceutical industry?***

**How it works in the pharmaceutical industry:** Description of types of innovations in the Walgreens pharmacy chain (Collins, 2001; Japsen, 2020; Knox, 2021; Russo, 2023; WBA, 2023) (Appendix C).

## Service innovation

- Calculating revenue per customer visit allowed Walgreens to improve service and expand its range of additional services, such as 'photo in an hour'.
- In the 1980s, Walgreens shared information access for all drugstores, turning the chain into a 'neighbourhood drugstore'.
- The opening of a drive-in pharmacy in the 1990s was similar to that of McDonald's restaurants.
- In 1999, a website was created where customers could place orders online, refill prescriptions, receive recommendations from pharmacists, participate in loyalty programmes, etc.
- Walgreens became the first drugstore chain to offer prescription labels in multiple languages.

- The mobile application created in 2010 made it possible to refill prescriptions quickly, receive reminders about taking medications, and provide pharmaceutical care online.
- Walgreens offers telemedicine services, which is especially important during pandemics (COVID-19).
- The integrated use of digital tools allows Walgreens to improve the pharmacy's CX continuously.
- Walgreens has integrated various healthcare services for patients by opening Walgreens healthcare clinics, etc.

**Technology innovation**

- Implementing the Intercom electronic network in the 1980s allowed Walgreens to consolidate customer information into one information centre.
- Walgreens was the first in the drugstore market to use a computerised inventory control system, scanners, etc.
- Walgreens is the first retailer to test drone delivery.
- The company was among the first in the drugstore market to create an Internet website and, later, a mobile application.
- In 2020, Walgreens launched a strategic partnership with Microsoft and Adobe to create a new personalised platform to enhance CX.
- Walgreens uses digital tools, robotics, and other IT tools to improve pharmacy formats, customer service, etc. For example, Walgreens developed approximately 100 in-house AI solutions.

**Business process innovation**

- Charles Walgreen focused the company's development on the pharmacy business with a new 'corner drugstore' format.
- The innovative implementation of the Intercom, scanning system, etc. has improved the company's logistics and interaction with suppliers.
- Walgreens has built its ecosystem in partnership with healthcare providers, insurers, and digital health companies: more than 400 Walgreens clinics in the United States, hundreds of testing centres in pharmacies, omnichannel customer interactions (offline and online), etc.
- In 2014, Walgreens was the first to enter the international market under the WBA brand, integrating healthcare, pharmacy, and retail.

- Walgreens is innovating in education and wellness for its associates by creating Walgreens University, an online portal for continuing professional education, and a mental health and wellness programme.
- Walgreens has transformed its approach to evaluating leadership and management: bonuses are awarded not only for financial achievements but also for team members' involvement in customer service and participation in the community's events and activities.

## 6.4 Conclusions

1 Ethical principles regulate the norms of behaviour and interaction of people in organisations. A leader's adherence to ethical standards in pharmacy is reflected in their intentions, actions, and behaviour in creating values for patients, employees, partners, communities, and other stakeholders. A leader's ethics is based on moral maturity, moral values, and adherence to ethical leadership principles: respect others, show justice, manifest honesty, build community, and serve others.

2 The lack of moral and ethical guidelines in pharmaceutical leaders can not only negatively affect the company's sustainable development but also threaten patients' health and well-being. Such leaders are destructive, guided only by personal interests, create an organisational culture and values based on deception and manipulation, and force their managers and employees to demonstrate unethical and immoral behaviour while achieving organisational goals.

3 Innovation in the pharmaceutical industry is a crucial factor in winning and maintaining leadership positions in the market. This involves the creation of not only innovative healthcare products but also innovative types of services, technologies, and business processes. All these types of innovations must be interconnected and integrated. The leader is responsible for implementing innovations and creating and maintaining an organisational culture that encourages innovativeness, creativity, and a collaborative approach.

## References

Al-Madhagi, H.A., (2023). FDA-approved drugs in 2022: A brief outline. *Saudi Pharmaceutical Journal: SPJ: the Official Publication of the Saudi Pharmaceutical Society*, 31(3), 401–409. https://doi.org/10.1016/j.jsps.2023.01.007

Arnold, D.G., Amato, L.H., Troyer, J.L., & Stewart, O.J., (2022). Innovation and misconduct in the pharmaceutical industry. *Journal of Business Research*, 144, 1052–1063. https://doi.org/10.1016/j.jbusres.2022.02.026

Beauchamp, T.L., & Bowie, N.E., (1988). *Ethical Theory and Business*. 9th edition. Englewood Cliffs, NJ: Prentice Hall.

Bower, M., (1997). *The Will to Lead*. Boston, MA: Harvard Business School Press.

Burns, J.M., (1978). *Leadership*. New York: Harper & Row.

Burns, J.M., (2003). *Transforming Leadership: A New Pursuit of Happiness*. New York: Atlantic Monthly Pr.

Collins, J., (2001). Level 5 leadership. The triumph of humility and fierce resolve. *Harvard Business Review*, 79(1), 66–175.

Demeter, K., (2023). Key drivers of business process innovation: The role of strategic focuses and product innovation. *Vezetéstudomány/Budapest Management Review*, 54(11), 15–27. https://doi.org/10.14267/VEZTUD.2023.11.02

Eban, K., (2019). *Bottle of Lies: The Inside Story of the Generic Drug Boom*. New York: Ecco Press.

Forbes, (n.d.). *Quote by Albert Schweitzer*. Forbes. Available from: https://www.forbes.com/quotes/222/ [Accessed 17 May 2024].

Gambardella, A., (1995). *Science and Innovation: The US Pharmaceutical Industry during the 1980s*. New York: Cambridge University Press.

Green, S., (2008). Ethics and the pharmaceutical industry. *Australasian Psychiatry*, 16 (3), 158–165. https://journals.sagepub.com/doi/10.1080/10398560701842595

Japsen, B., (2020). Walgreens Partners with Adobe and Microsoft to 'Personalize' Customer Experience. *Forbes* [online], 30 June 2020. Available from: https://www.forbes.com/sites/brucejapsen/2020/06/30/walgreens-partners-with-adobe-and-microsoft-to-personalize-customer-experience/ [Accessed 04 February 2024].

Klein, S., (2000). Drucker as business moralist. *Journal of Business Ethics*, 28(2), 121–128. https://doi.org/10.1023/A:1006222808524

Kleinman, P., (2013). *Philosophy 101: From Plato and Socrates to Ethics and Metaphysics, an Essential Primer on the History of Thought*. Avon, MA: Adams Media.

Knox, D., (2021). How Walgreens Boots Alliance Is Embracing an Entrepreneurial Mindset. *Forbes* [online], 8 April 2021. Available from: https://www.forbes.com/sites/daveknox/2021/04/08/how-walgreens-boots-alliance-is-embracing-an-entrepreneurial-mindset/ [Accessed 05 February 2024].

Kohlberg, L., (1984). *Essays on Moral Development, Vol. 2: The Psychology of Moral Development*. New York: Harper & Row.

Kouzes, J.M., & Posner, B.Z., (1987). *The Leadership Challenge: How to Get Extraordinary Things Done in Organizations*. San Francisco, CA: Jossey-Bass.

Lou, L.L., Flood, A., Yang, T., Whitley, R.J., (2022). Commentary: John C. Martin (1951–2021). *Antiviral Therapy*, 27(2). https://journals.sagepub.com/doi/full/10.1177/13596535211067895

Northouse, P.G., (2021). *Leadership: Theory and Practice*. 9th edition. Los Angeles, CA: Sage Publications.

OECD, (2010). *The OECD Innovation Strategy: Getting a Head Start on Tomorrow – France OECD*. [online]. Available from: https://www.oecd.org/en/publications/2010/05/the-oecd-innovation-strategy_g1ghcb7c.html [Accessed 10 February 2024].

Padilla, A., Hogan, R., & Kaiser, R.B., (2007). The toxic triangle: Destructive leaders, susceptible followers, and conducive environments. *The Leadership Quarterly*, 18, 176–194. https://doi.org/10.1016/j.leaqua.2007.03.001

Rawls, J., (1971). *A Theory of Justice*. Boston, MA: Harvard University Press.

Russo, E., (2023). WBA Wins Gold Stevie Award for Most Innovative Company of the Year. *WBA* [online], 28 April 2023. Available from: https://www.walgreensbootsalliance.com/news-media/our-stories/wba-wins-gold-stevie-award-most-innovative-company-year [Accessed 30 January 2024].

Santoro, M.A., & Gorrie, T.M., (2005). *Ethics and the Pharmaceutical Industry*. New York: Cambridge University Press.

Vagelos, P.R., & Galambos, L., (2006). *The Moral Corporation - Merck Experiences*. New York: Cambridge University Press.

WBA, (2023). *History of Walgreens Boots Alliance*. Walgreens Boots Alliance, Inc. [online]. Available from: https://www.walgreensbootsalliance.com/about-us/history [Accessed 30 January 2024].

Welch, J., & Welch, S., (2005). *Winning*. New York: Harper Business.

Writer, S., (2021). Pfizer CEO Albert Bourla: How digital played a role in the 'impossible task' of vaccine production. *Marketing–Interactive* [online], 30 April, 2021. Available from: https://www.marketing-interactive.com/pfizer-ceo-albert-bourla-how-digital-played-a-role-in-the-impossible-task-of-vaccine-production [Accessed 18 January 2024].

# 7 Leadership and organisational culture in the pharmaceutical industry

## 7.1 Basic foundations of organisational culture

Organisational culture reflects the leader's vision for the company's development and the employees' willingness to accept and share its core principles. There is a seven-dimension Organizational Culture Profile (OCP), which defines the thinking and behaviour model of the leader and employees (O'Reilly et al., 1991):

- ***Innovation and risk-taking*** – to what extent the organisation's employees are ready and prepared for innovation and risk.
  The pharmaceutical industry is one of the most innovative in the world, so the most influential leaders understand the importance of investing in creating new medicines despite the high risks. For example, the Novartis Institutes for Biomedical Research makes all the conditions for scientists' full-fledged work and fruitful cooperation with research laboratories, academic centres, etc. to create revolutionary drug therapy (Armstrong, 2009).
- ***Attention to detail*** – how much precision, meticulousness, and attention to detail are required from employees.
  The activities of pharmaceutical companies are strictly regulated; for example, pre-clinical trials and clinical trials, as well as the production, promotion, and distribution of drugs, must be carried out following GxP. Therefore, employees are usually required to be precise, meticulous, and attentive to detail.
- ***Outcome orientation*** – the extent to which a leader pays attention to the result rather than the methods and processes used to achieve it.
  Prominent pharmaceutical leaders have always focused on delivering value to all stakeholders, especially patients. However, suppose a company leader is only focused on maximising profits. In that case, this can lead to serious misconduct, such as the opioid crisis in the US and the bankruptcy of Ranbaxy.
- ***People orientation*** – to what extent the organisation considers the interests of employees and their development.

DOI: 10.4324/9781003617266-8

Leaders should pay attention to employees' interests and development to increase their motivation and involvement in achieving organisational goals. For example, Paul Janssen organised the functioning of the Janssen Pharmaceutica laboratory to meet the needs and scientific interests of scientists, creating the necessary conditions for increasing their internal motivation.

- ***Team orientation*** – the extent to which the organisation's functioning is centred around team groups rather than individuals.
  Successful companies maintain a sustainable balance between individual attention and teamwork. Albert Bourla highlighted that the success in creating a COVID-19 vaccine in record time was due to the efforts of his team and all Pfizer employees (Whipple, 2022).
- ***Aggressiveness*** – the extent to which employees act more aggressively and competitively than in a more relaxed manner.
  To achieve the desired result, it is vital to adequately assess the current situation, considering the analysis of own capabilities and resources, competitive advantages, etc. Vasella believed the organisation should use a more rigid and competitive behaviour style to succeed. However, he also recognised the need for adaptability, as seen in his efforts to minimise the pressure associated with achieving short-term goals in the research division of Novartis.
- ***Stability*** – the extent to which the organisation is focused on maintaining the status quo rather than striving for growth and development.
  For outstanding leaders in the pharmaceutical industry, the status quo is not a leadership approach. Instead, they focus on innovation, finding new opportunities to meet the needs of patients in terms of health and well-being. Equally important is their adherence to the vision of the organisation's development and their actions in line with organisational values. This not only fosters a sense of confidence in the future, stability, and security among employees but also underscores the key responsibility of leaders.

According to Schein and Schein (2017), organisational culture is a multi-layered concept, with each level having a unique impact on employees and the organisation as a whole. These levels vary in the degree of influence on employees, visibility, and publicity. The arrangement of these levels can be compared to an iceberg, where the top represents the visible level of organisational culture – ***artifacts***, under the surface – ***espoused beliefs and values***, and in the depths – ***underlying assumptions***.

***Artifacts***, the visible elements of organisational culture, are just the tip of the iceberg when it comes to understanding any company. These include the design of premises, the technologies used, brand attributes, the appearance and manner of communication of employees, the proclaimed vision, mission, and values of the company, etc. The characteristic feature of this level is that it gives only a superficial idea of the organisational culture.

The next level – ***espoused beliefs and values*** – covers almost all areas of the organisation's functioning: procedures, rules, standards, features of personnel motivation and promotion, methods of conflict resolution, priority of task execution, etc. Leaders generally form espoused beliefs and values that correspond to their system of values, perceptions, and expectations in many ways. However, the organisation's members' shared acceptance of these 'built-in' values and beliefs transforms them into internal norms and standards.

Over time, the organisational culture formed under the leader's influence is significantly shaped by employees' perceptions, which in turn influence their behaviour, thoughts, and expectations at a deeper level. This process determines the third level of culture – ***underlying assumptions***. Deep values and beliefs can reflect the attitude towards the leader, the employees' perception of their role in the organisation, and other organisational issues; for example, 'the leader's decisions are not discussed and are carried out unconditionally', 'our proposals are important and valuable to the management', 'everyone is for themselves here', and so on.

It is worth noting that an organisation is characterised not only by a ***dominant*** organisational culture but also by ***subcultures*** formed at various levels of the company. The larger the organisation, the more subcultures it has: for example, global corporations such as Pfizer, Novartis, or Merck are also characterised by subcultures of regional offices, which are influenced by various national characteristics, language, business environment, and other factors. The stronger an organisational culture is, the more effectively it is integrated with the subcultures, beliefs, and values held by employees.

A ***strong organisational culture***, according to Schein and Schein (2017), should have the following characteristics: ***structural stability*** – to form a sense of stability, certainty, and significance of elements of organisational culture in employees; ***depth*** – not only to have external and superficial manifestations but also to influence deep patterns of employees' behaviour; ***breadth*** – to cover all aspects of the organisation's functioning, features of interaction with both internal and external stakeholders, making everyone feel included and involved; ***integrity*** – elements of organisational culture should be interconnected and reinforce each other's actions to achieve organisational goals.

The most influential leaders in the pharmaceutical industry created a strong organisational culture that significantly impacted people's behaviour even after they left leadership positions in the company. Their influence is not a thing of the past. John C. Martin's culture, which is focused on high standards, creating maximum patient value, and developing new leaders, is still felt. Paul Janssen's organisational values for continuous professional development, science orientation, and high performance continue to shape the industry. Charles Walgreen's emphasis on innovativeness, high service, and customer focus is an ongoing force.

**Food for thought:** ***What should a leader do to build a strong organisational culture?***

**How it works in the pharmaceutical industry:** Description of the organisational culture dimensions of Pfizer under the leadership of Albert Bourla during the COVID-19 pandemic (Appendix D).

### Innovation and risk-taking – High level

Creating a COVID-19 vaccine in the shortest possible time using new and unproven mRNA technology was a massive risk for the company. In addition to product and technology innovations, Pfizer made significant investments in organisational innovations. These included creating mobile manufacturing facilities, transportation solutions, and more. These investments demonstrated the company's commitment to overcoming challenges and achieving its goals and contributed to the launch of the antiviral drug Paxlovid.

### Attention to detail – High/middle level

Considering that the creation of a vaccine takes up to 10 years on average, the development of the COVID-19 vaccine was carried out using a simplified procedure, which does not allow for all the necessary details related to the phased introduction of the drug to the market. However, even in this expedited process, the importance of attention to detail cannot be overstated. As Albert Bourla noted, producing a vaccine on a global population scale requires meticulous care and precision, ensuring the quality and safety of the vaccine (Whipple, 2022).

### Outcome orientation – High level

Albert Bourla and his team did everything possible to achieve the desired result, directing all available resources and the potential of employees to solve problems related to the development of a vaccine against COVID-19. Conditions for fruitful cooperation with external stakeholders were also created: The Global COVID-19 Medical Service Program was organised to involve doctors, and Pfizer opened access to its technologies, such as viral screening and cell-based assays, for this united cause (National Journal, n.d.).

**People orientation – Low level**

The intense focus on the task at hand overshadowed the consideration of employees' needs and creating a comfortable working environment. Many people worked beyond their limits, went months without seeing their families, and were unable to be with loved ones who were sick with COVID-19. However, Pfizer employees remained intrinsically motivated and enthusiastic about developing a vaccine because they understood the significance of their mission.

**Team orientation – Middle/high level**

Following Albert Bourla's decision to begin developing a vaccine, a SWAT team of 11 highly qualified employees, including chemists, virologists, biologists, pharmacologists, and others, was assembled (National Journal, n.d.). Teamwork and integrating knowledge and skills from different fields made competent and timely management decisions possible. All Pfizer employees worked harmoniously and effectively, setting aside personal ambitions to achieve a common goal.

**Aggressiveness – High level**

The pharmaceutical market is highly competitive, often necessitating tough decisions. During the COVID-19 pandemic, the situation became even more complex and unpredictable. As Albert Bourla later noted, he had to be quite harsh and unyielding towards employees who faced doubts or difficulties in solving critical problems. However, despite these challenging situations, solutions were found that allowed the team to move forward (Whipple, 2022).

**Stability – Low level**

Despite the high level of uncertainty and risk involved in developing a COVID-19 vaccine, Pfizer employees felt stability and confidence in their leader, Albert Bourla, in being part of an industry-leading company with vast resources, capabilities, and talented people. The organisational values that inspired them to be bold, execute with excellence, uphold ethical principles, and tackle ambitious and complex challenges further reinforced their commitment.

## 7.2 Elements of organisational culture

Organisational culture consists of interrelated elements that various researchers have addressed: organisational values, communication and relationship culture, organisational climate, myths and stories, rituals and ceremonies, symbols and attributes (Schein & Schein, 2017).

***Organisational values*** are not just standards but crucial guidelines for the organisation to steer its activities. These values play a significant role in determining the behaviour of employees and shaping their daily actions and decisions. They also play a key role in outlining the company's primary obligations to its stakeholders. For instance, Janssen Pharmaceutica, the pharmaceutical division of Johnson & Johnson, prioritises its responsibility to patients, healthcare professionals, and all consumers of its products, followed by its commitments to employees, communities, and shareholders.

***The culture of communication and relationships*** depends not only on the organisation's leader but also on their team, with whom they form the organisational culture. For new employees who have just joined the company, understanding and accepting the specifics of relationships within the team is essential, especially for their quick and successful adaptation to the team. The culture of communication and relationships can include the following aspects:

- Emphasis on formal or less formal communication both with colleagues and with management.
- Using specific terms, proprietary 'corporate expressions', and nonverbal communication.
- Features of relationships between employees from different departments.
- Features of responding to conflict situations and ways to resolve them.
- Relationships based on respecting the individuality of each employee or striving to 'educate' them according to certain norms and standards.

Even though each company's communication culture is unique, prominent leaders in the pharmaceutical industry formed it in a way that allowed them to achieve their goals effectively.

***The organisational climate*** significantly impacts the culture of communication and relationships. A healthy and positive environment is rooted in an atmosphere of trust. To achieve this, it is essential to ensure the 'transparency' of the management system, which includes clarity and consistency of goals and fairness in distributing tasks, resources, and rewards. Additionally, clear rules, procedures, and standards must regulate the requirements for functional organisational processes. Trust, particularly in a leader, is crucial since its absence can greatly demotivate employees and hinder their ability to achieve their goals.

***Myths and stories*** are integral to organisational culture. They are the stories of the company's creation, transformation, iconic products or services, and the significant contributions of its leaders and employees. These narratives play a crucial role in the socialisation of new employees, helping them understand the company's values, norms, and history. They strengthen team spirit, promote employee involvement, and inspire new employees, making them feel part of the organisational culture.

***Rituals and ceremonies*** are the fabric that binds the team together. Rituals are everyday and often programmed features of a team's life. For example, the work schedule, break time and its content, frequency, and specifics of routine communication with management, colleagues, clients, etc. Ceremonies include the specifics of holding official and unofficial work and cultural events.

***Symbols and attributes*** are crucial in creating a sense of belonging to the organisation and its values among employees. These elements of organisational culture, such as corporate clothing style, corporate symbols, awards, interior design, and signs with employee regalia, are not just the organisation's 'calling card' but also underscore employees' status. They are particularly significant during organisational transformations or when employees are set complex and ambitious goals. For example, the slogan '*Science will win*' became an inspiring symbol for Pfizer employees, motivating them to persevere in creating a vaccine against COVID-19. Albert Bourla and his employees wore face masks and T-shirts with the inscription 'Science will win'; it was distributed as the hashtag #ScienceWillWin on social networks, etc. (National Journal, n.d.). This symbol of corporate victory has become woven into Pfizer's organisational culture, inspiring and motivating thousands of Pfizer employees worldwide.

**Food for thought: *Which elements of organisational culture are most important?***

**How it works in the pharmaceutical industry:** Description of the organisational culture elements of the Janssen Pharmaceutica research laboratory under the leadership of Paul Janssen (Appendix A).

## Organisational values

Paul Janssen's renowned phrase, 'The patients are waiting' (Gurowitz, 2015), is more than a slogan. It reflects the practical application of his patient-oriented concept. Dr Paul expected his team to embody his fundamental values in their work: continuous critical analysis, courage in implementing their ideas, and a focus on creating patentable inventions.

## The culture of communication and relationships

The interaction between employees in the Janssen Pharmaceutica laboratory was based on common scientific interests and a joint search for solutions to problems. The communication culture was based on cooperation, and Paul Janssen, like an orchestra conductor, coordinated the work of specialists from various functional areas. As a leader, Dr Paul did not try to 'educate' his employees but encouraged them to pursue their scientific interests (Lewi & Smith, 2007).

## The organisational climate

The organisational climate in the research centre was built on trust and mutual respect, two key pillars that Paul Janssen believed were essential for a thriving research environment. Janssen's philosophy was that researchers did not need to be controlled. He believed they should be given freedom and the necessary resources and opportunities to realise their scientific interests. Clear and understandable expectations from employees in the laboratory, which consisted of creating patentable inventions, further enhanced the healthy climate for the team (Lewi & Smith, 2007).

## Myths and stories

Since Janssen Pharmaceutica was founded in 1953, numerous myths and stories have been woven into its organisational culture; one of them, for example, is connected with the creation of haloperidol in 1958. Thus, as a result of testing one of the compounds for analgesic effect, its antipsychotic properties were discovered. After that, Dr Paul offered a copy of the drug to a famous psychiatrist, who successfully used a few milligrams on a patient with severe psychosis. Soon, haloperidol became available to a wide range of patients. This medicine changed the duration of hospitalisation and treatment of patients, became the golden standard of antipsychotics, and was also one of the WHO's List of Essential Medicines (Granger & Albu, 2005).

**Rituals and ceremonies**

One of the most famous rituals was Paul Janssen's tour of the research centre. Dr Paul could be found in one of the many corridors of the laboratory asking, 'What is new?' Typically, Janssen would begin his tour of those labs that had interesting news, according to the morning briefing. The lab staff had prepared their results several days earlier in tables and graphs, allowing for effective discussion. Afterwards, Paul Janssen would advise the employees and inspire them to push the boundaries further. Formal meetings were not held in the lab. Dr Paul would decide to hold them only if he and the scientists had no consensus (Lewi & Smith, 2007).

**Symbols and attributes**

The most important symbol in the research centre was its legendary founder and director, Paul Janssen. Throughout his life, he received numerous awards, including five honorary professorships and 22 honorary doctorates, and became one of the most productive researchers in developing new medicinal compounds. In 2004, the Dr Paul Janssen Award for Biomedical Research was established to recognise and encourage the contributions of talented scientists to improving human health. Many award recipients have also become Nobel laureates (Johnson & Johnson, n.d.).

## 7.3 Leader's role in the organisational culture

Organisational culture begins to form when a company is created, with the leader playing a fundamental role in this process. Employees also significantly impact the strengthening of organisational culture. If the culture meets their expectations and values, they will gradually become its bearers. The organisation's subsequent development is typically associated with new employees who bring their values and expectations. The process of the evolution of organisational culture is illustrated in Figure 7.1.

***The beliefs, values, and expectations of a leader*** significantly impact a company as they lay the foundation for its future development. Paul Janssen, for instance, not only spent his entire life doing what was his passion and hobby but also inspired his employees to develop professionally, be bold, and be proactive in creating new drugs. As he noted: 'Research workers must stimulate one another intellectually. Research must be their hobby. What is nicer than being able to earn your living by practicing your hobby?' (Gurowitz, 2015).

*Figure 7.1* Sources of organisational culture and its evolution.

It's important to note that organisational culture, whether positive or negative, significantly influences ***employees' learning experience***. A striking example is the case of the Indian pharmaceutical company Ranbaxy, which ceased to exist due to systemic violations in drug research, testing, and production. Following this, its leading employees transitioned to other companies. Notably, after former Ranbaxy top manager Rajiv Malik assumed the role of president at the American pharmaceutical company Mylan, the focus shifted from patient interests to profit maximisation. This shift led to Mylan facing accusations of drug quality, data unreliability with the FDA, and collusion in inflating generic drug prices (Eban, 2019).

Organisational culture is of particular importance when new team members appear who need to socialise, that is, understand and accept the main visible aspects of this culture, the existing pitfalls. Ultimately, ***new employees' beliefs, values, and expectations*** are woven into the organisational culture. When the Belgian colony in Africa gained independence in the 1960s, many scientists returned to Belgium. Paul Janssen invited them to work at the Janssen Pharmaceutica research centre: 'Come to work here, we have a lot to do' (Lewi, n.d., p. 5). New employees brought their values, expectations, scientific ideas, and interests to the company, which were successfully woven into the organisational culture of the laboratory.

According to Schein and Schein (2017), several mechanisms allow a leader to embed his beliefs, values, and assumptions into the company's organisational culture.

- ***What leaders pay attention to, measure, and control on a regular basis.*** Paul Janssen, John C. Martin, Charles Cork Walgreen III, and other outstanding leaders in the pharmaceutical industry were deeply committed to creating value for patients as their primary stakeholders. Dr Janssen expected high employee performance and innovative solutions in synthesising new chemical compounds. John C. Martin closely monitored patient needs while developing innovative and high-quality drugs. Charles Cork Walgreen III consistently oversaw the implementation of tasks to make the pharmacy chain highly convenient and profitable per customer visit.

- ***How leaders react to critical incidents and organisational crises.***
  Business leaders who have achieved incredible results never give up and are persistent in achieving goals, inspiring and motivating their team and other employees. Albert Bourla faced numerous problems and challenges many times during the development of the COVID-19 vaccine. At the same time, he motivated his employees to find the best way out of the current situation. Here is what Bourla said about his employees: 'You will be surprised how much they can do if you don't relax the target. If you tell him it is what it is, go and find a solution. They may not do it exactly. But they will do 10 times more than what you thought they would' (Fleischmann, 2022).
- ***How leaders allocate resources.***
  To achieve both short-term and long-term goals, leaders in the pharmaceutical industry invested in the company's development, looking for new opportunities and prospects. Having become CEO of Walgreens, Charles Walgreen III decided to fully concentrate on the pharmacy business and actively invest in innovations, open new pharmacies, expand the range of additional services, etc. As a result, he created a strong organisational culture focused on customers, a commitment to innovation, and the professionalism of employees.
- ***Deliberate role modelling, teaching, and coaching.***
  Leaders of successful companies demonstrate the desired organisational behaviour model by their example. John C. Martin's constant contact with vital stakeholders such as doctors and patients to obtain valuable feedback, and his active involvement of his team members in this process, and Paul Janssen's emphasis on the value of courage in conducting scientific research, which he believed was no less important than competence and professionalism, and his motivation of his employees to develop their competencies, scientific thinking, and openness to new ideas, are all valuable lessons for leaders. As Janssen stated, 'The human mind is like a parachute. It works best when it is open' (Gurowitz, 2015).
- ***How leaders allocate rewards and status.***
  The successful development of an organisation depends on aligning external motivation factors with its vision, strategy, and goals. This alignment, together with the elements of organisational culture, is key to creating an environment that empowers employees to implement their ideas and create tangible value for patients. Albert Bourla, a proponent of this approach, consistently aimed to build a culture at Pfizer where initiative, enthusiasm, and effectiveness were the primary criteria for rewards and status allocation. Furthermore, all influential leaders in the pharmaceutical industry understand that no external incentives can drive people to work beyond

their capabilities if they are not inspired and enthusiastic about achieving a socially significant and ambitious goal.

- ***How leaders recruit, select, promote, and excommunicate.*** Successful companies recruit and promote staff following an organisational culture based on clear and understandable values which employees perceive as fair and inspiring. For instance, the Paul Janssen Research Center recruited staff based on talent and professional competence. Dr Paul believed that the laboratory should be adapted to the needs and scientific interests of the researchers rather than the other way around. This philosophy resonates with the importance of an employee-centric approach in recruitment and promotion.

The leader's effective interaction with the management team is crucial in maintaining and strengthening the values and beliefs contributing to the organisation's goals. The human resources (HR) director (manager) and the HR department play a prominent role in this process. Their functions, including selection, development, training, remuneration of personnel, as well as their adaptation, are integral to the full development of human capital. For example, Albert Bourla noted that HR is one of the most critical functions in an organisation, which requires special attention, especially with the advent of new IT (Gurchiek, 2021).

In crises, which are usually caused by the influence of environmental factors, the leader can carry out organisational transformations. However, cardinal changes in strategy, goals, systems functioning, and processes can be successful only if they correlate with the company's organisational culture. Otherwise, it is necessary to change the organisational value system.

**Food for thought:** ***Which traits and competencies should a leader possess to transform organisational culture?***

**How it works in the pharmaceutical industry:** Description of organisational culture formation mechanisms on the example of Daniel Vasella's leadership (Appendix E).

### What leaders pay attention to, measure, and control on a regular basis

As the leader of Novartis, Daniel Vasella focused on how the company creates value for key stakeholders. Improving patient well-being and healthcare standards became Novartis's primary goals. Vasella emphasised that while financial results are significant – since the company cannot survive without them – money is not the primary objective. As he exclaimed: 'is our purpose to make rich people richer or to discover better medicines for people who suffer? For us it is the latter' (Forbes, 2009).

## How leaders react to critical incidents and organisational crises

Like any company, Novartis faced various challenges, such as a decline in sales, an unsuccessful launch of a new drug, problems with patent protection, etc., but this did not stop Daniel Vasella from moving forward. For example, he initiated the 'Forward Initiative' programme, which implied organisational structure changes, reducing bureaucratic procedures to increase Novartis's competitiveness, productivity, and adaptability (Armstrong, 2009).

## How leaders allocate resources

Vasella consistently emphasised the importance of research and innovation for Novartis's successful and sustainable development. To shift the company's focus from synthesising chemical compounds to creating biological healthcare products, Vasella invested $4 billion in the Institute for Biomedical Research and moved Novartis's global R&D headquarters from Basel to Cambridge, Massachusetts (Armstrong, 2009). He also differentiated the business by successfully investing in developing original drugs and other healthcare products.

## Deliberate role modelling, teaching, and coaching

Daniel Vasella demonstrated commitment to organisational values by personal example. He viewed his role as motivating people to achieve clear, ambitious, and inspiring goals while also identifying their strengths and nurturing new leaders. Novartis initiated various programmes for personnel development, including for top managers, to foster a commitment to developing new knowledge, skills, and continuous self-improvement. As Vasella noted, 'Few things are as fulfilling as seeing top people grow to the next level of leadership contribution' (Cashman, 2013).

### How leaders allocate rewards and status

Upon his appointment as Novartis CEO, Daniel Vasella made it clear that exceptional performance would be generously rewarded. The company set explicit targets and incentives for top achievers, with Vasella emphasising specific outcomes as the basis for recognition. He also fostered an environment that allowed scientists to engage in long-term research, as evidenced by his direct oversight of the Novartis Institute for Biomedical Research, where Dr Mark Fishman, its President, reported directly to him (Armstrong, 2009).

### How leaders recruit, select, promote, and excommunicate

Daniel Vasella paid considerable attention to recruitment at Novartis, focusing not only on candidates' professional knowledge and skills but also their values. It was important for the company to select people motivated to develop innovative medicinal therapies. On average, Vasella participated in about 50 interviews annually for managerial positions (Betov & Szillat, 2016). He also emphasised the importance of employees' ability to improve economic indicators. For example, Vasella's successor in 2010 was Joseph Jimenez, the division head of Novartis Pharmaceuticals, who significantly reduced the company's expenses (Armstrong, 2009).

## 7.4 Conclusions

1 Organisational culture is a complex concept that shapes employees' behavioural patterns. It can be assessed in terms of innovation and risk-taking, attention to detail, people or team orientation, outcome orientation, aggressiveness, and stability. Organisational culture is characterised by levels that vary in their strength of influence and external visibility: artefacts, espoused beliefs and values, and underlying assumptions. The more deeply ingrained the values are in an organisational culture, the stronger that culture becomes.
2 Organisational culture consists of various integrated elements. Organisational values serve as behaviour guidelines and ethical standards. The communication culture reflects the specifics of interaction between the leader and the team. A healthy organisational climate is based on trust and transparency within the management system. Myths and stories help

strengthen team spirit and foster a sense of pride and involvement in the organisation. Rituals and ceremonies highlight the team's operational characteristics, while symbols and attributes reinforce employees' commitment to the organisation's values.

3 The leader's vision shapes the organisational culture, which the staff should perceive as fair and inspiring. New employees contribute to the evolution of the organisational culture, making it dynamic and adaptive. Leaders can use various mechanisms to embed their beliefs, values, and assumptions into the organisational culture, such as focusing on specific organisational indicators, responding to crises, setting priorities in resource allocation, and establishing systems for selection, remuneration, and promotion of personnel.

## References

Armstrong, W., (2009). The Book on Daniel. *Pharmaceutical Executive* [online], 01 October 2009. Available from: https://www.pharmexec.com/view/book-daniel [Accessed 22 February 2024].

Betov, A., & Szillat, P., (2016). Business leadership concepts exemplified by the two exceptional leaders Daniel Vasella and Ricardo Semler. *Journal of Contemporary Economic and Business Issues*, 3(1), 32–60.

Cashman, K., (2013). A Global Leader's Perspective on CEO Leadership: Part One. *Forbes* [online], 5 June 2013. Available from: https://www.forbes.com/sites/kevincashman/2013/04/18/a-global-leaders-perspective-on-ceo-leadership-part-one-2/ [Accessed 19 December 2023].

Eban, K., (2019). *Bottle of Lies: The Inside Story of the Generic Drug Boom*. New York: Ecco Press.

Fleischmann, A., (2022). Albert Bourla. Chairman and CEO, Pfizer. *Leadership Matters* [online], 05 April 2022. Available from: https://www.leadershipmattersshow.com/episodes/albert-bourla [Accessed 15 February 2024].

Forbes, (2009). Putting Patients at the Center of Innovation [online]. *Forbes*. Available from: https://www.forbes.com/2009/10/08/novartis-vasella-pharma-leadership-ceonetwork-managing.html [Accessed 24 February 2024].

Granger, B., & Albu, S., (2005). The haloperidol story. *Annals of Clinical Psychiatry*, 17(3), 137–140. doi: 10.1080/10401230591002048.

Gurchiek, K., (2021). Pfizer and SHRM CEOs Discuss COVID-19, Value of Culture. *SHRM* [online], 17 March 2021. Available from: https://www.shrm.org/topics-tools/news/pfizer-shrm-ceos-discuss-covid-19-value-culture [Accessed 16 February 2024].

Gurowitz, M., (2015). The legacy of Dr. Paul Janssen: How a "funny idea" helped change the course of modern medicine. *Johnson & Johnson* [online], 11 September 2015. Available from: https://www.jnj.com/the-legacy-of-dr-paul-janssen-how-a-funny-idea-helped-change-the-course-of-modern-medicine [Accessed 11 December 2023].

Johnson & Johnson, (n.d.). Dr Paul Janssen Award [online]. *Johnson & Johnson*. Available from: https://www.pauljanssenaward.com/ [Accessed 07 March 2024].

Lewi, P.J., (n.d.). Drug Design with Dr. Paul Janssen [online]. *DataScope*. Available from: https://www.datascope.be/Drug%20Design/English.pdf [Accessed 23 October 2023].

Lewi, P.J., & Smith, A., (2007). Successful pharmaceutical discovery: Paul Janssen's concept of drug research. *R&D Management*, 37(4), 355–362. https://doi.org/10.1111/j.1467-9310.2007.00481.x

National Journal, (n.d.). *Business leaders: Albert Bourla* [online]. National Journal. Available from: https://go.nationaljournal.com/rs/556-YEE-969/images/Business Leaders_Albert_Bourla.pdf [Accessed 10 August 2024].

O'Reilly, C., Chatman, I.I.I., & Caldwell, J., D.F., (1991). People and organisational culture: A profile comparison approach to assessing person organisation fit. *Academy of Management Journal*, 34(3), 487–516. https://www.jstor.org/stable/256404

Schein, E.H., & Schein, P.A., (2017). *Organisational Culture and Leadership*. 5th edition. San Francisco: Wiley & Sons.

Whipple, T., (2022). Billions at stake, endless waiting, an angry Trump: the Pfizer's CEO great vax hunt. *The Sydney Morning Herald*, 09 April 2022. Available from: https://www.smh.com.au/national/billions-at-stake-endless-waiting-an-angry-trump-the-pfizer-ceo-s-great-vax-hunt-20220304-p5a1q7.html [Accessed 25 February 2024].

# 8 Leadership, strategy, and organisational changes in the pharmaceutical industry

## 8.1 Basic foundations of organisational strategy

A leader's vision for an organisation's development is not just an intention but a result when put into practice. As American author and researcher Joel A. Barker noted: 'Vision without action is merely a dream. Action without vision just passes the time. Vision with action can change the world' (Ratcliffe, 2016). This change occurs when the leader and their team collaborate to develop a strategy for implementing the organisation's vision.

The organisational ***strategy*** is an action plan for how a company achieves its vision and goals. The importance of strategy is difficult to overestimate, but at the same time, its effectiveness depends on several factors:

- The ability of a leader and managers to assess their strengths, capabilities, and the influence of environmental factors, as Collins (2001) noted that companies should confront the brutal facts.
- The availability of an open and friendly climate in an organisation that contributes to the best options for implementing the strategy.
- The leader's readiness to listen to their team members, admit their own mistakes, and make decisions based on various judgments.
- The priority of long-term development of the organisation and its adaptation to constantly changing factors in the external environment.

Strategy can be viewed from the perspective of the following two areas: determining the company's market positioning to differentiate it from competitors and forming an approach to creating value for customers as the main stakeholders of the organisation (Aliekperov, 2021). The outstanding researcher in business strategy, Michael Porter, noted that 'the essence of strategy is choosing to perform an activity differently than rivals do' (Aliekperov, 2021, p. 3). At the same time, he emphasised that the company should determine how it will form a value proposition for its customers.

For example, Paul Janssen positioned his laboratory in terms of synthesising drugs of various pharmacological groups, including neuroleptics,

DOI: 10.4324/9781003617266-9

analgesics, antifungals, antiparasitic, gastrointestinal, and cardiovascular. His team of specialists with unique scientific interests was instrumental in this. After Janssen Pharmaceutica became part of the global company Johnson & Johnson, the drugs developed in Dr Paul Janssen's research centre became accessible to patients worldwide. According to Porter's matrix (see Section 8.2), Janssen Pharmaceutica adopted the differentiation leadership strategy, focusing on both a wide range of drugs and numerous sales markets. Meanwhile, Paul Janssen focused on creating unique patient value through innovative medicines.

From the perspective of a company's market positioning and value creation for customers, two types of strategies can be distinguished: corporate and business. The effective integration of these two approaches supports the organisation's sustainable development in alignment with its vision, mission, and values (Aliekperov, 2021) (see Figure 8.1).

***Corporate strategy*** defines the scope of a company's activities in relation to the industries and markets in which it plans to compete. Corporate strategy decisions include investments in diversification, vertical integration, mergers and acquisitions, and more. To determine the corporate strategy, a leader and their team must answer the question: 'Where?'

When John C. Martin became CEO of the biopharmaceutical company Gilead Sciences, he focused on a specific market segment – antiviral drugs for treating HIV, hepatitis B, hepatitis C, and other conditions. Under Martin's leadership, several acquisitions were made that strengthened the company's market position; among the most significant was the acquisition of Pharmasset, Inc. for $11 billion in 2011. This successful deal enabled Gilead Sciences

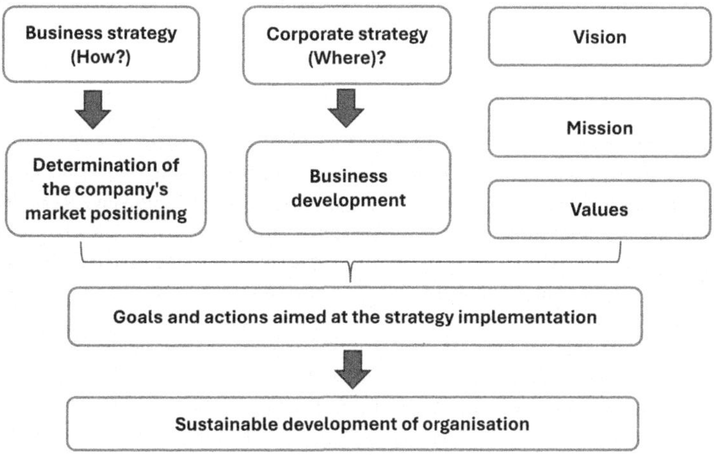


*Figure 8.1* Formation of organisational strategy.

to launch a unique, innovative drug, Sovaldi, for treating hepatitis C in 2013 (Gilead, 2022).

***Business strategy*** describes how a company creates its competitive advantages. To define a business strategy, a leader and their team must answer the question: 'How?' Most leaders in the pharmaceutical industry use a business strategy focused on creating innovative and unique products. Some companies, such as Gilead Sciences, concentrate on specific market segments – like antiviral drugs, which are indispensable to patients due to their unique characteristics. Other companies, such as Pfizer, Novartis, and Merck, compete across multiple product segments, including veterinary products, generic drugs, and biosimilars, employing various business strategies. Pharmaceutical companies that produce generic drugs typically adopt 'cost leadership' as their business strategy (see Section 8.2).

Creating value for stakeholders, particularly customers, is the cornerstone of any strategy aimed at sustainable development. As Porter (1985, p. 3) noted, 'Competitive advantage grows fundamentally out of value a firm is able to create for its buyers'. This requires that business and corporate strategies, along with organisational goals, be integrated with the company's vision, mission, and values.

The ***vision*** reflects the desired future image of the company. A vision has an inspiring effect on employees; it touches their emotions and hopes, raises standards of behaviour, and promotes the unification of people's efforts, knowledge, and skills in bringing it to reality. As the legendary Jack Welch noted, 'Leaders make sure people not only see the vision, they live and breathe it' (Welch & Welch, 2005, p. 67). The vision guides the organisation's development over five, ten, or more years. For example, according to Pfizer's new Blueprint adopted in 2023, its vision (ambition) for the next five years is to 'Change a billion lives a year'. Albert Bourla emphasised that to achieve this vision, the company will focus on reducing bureaucratic procedures, optimising functional processes, increasing adaptability, and more, leading to significant changes and improvements in its operations (Pfizer, 2023a).

A ***mission*** defines an organisation's primary purpose and its responsibility towards customers and society. When formulating a mission, it's crucial to briefly and concisely convey to stakeholders why the company exists, its advantages, and how its activities can improve people's lives. A leader must focus the organisation on its mission. For example, Pfizer's mission is 'Breakthroughs that change patients' lives'. 'Breakthroughs' signifies innovation; 'change' reflects the desire to radically improve patients' lives; and 'patients' lives' highlights the goal of creating value for patients, their families, and everyone they interact with (Pfizer, 2024).

***Organisational values*** reflect the foundational principles of an organisation's culture and serve as a moral compass for employees. Schein and Schein (2017, p. 30) noted, 'Such beliefs and values often become embodied in an ideology or organisational philosophy, which then serves as a guide to dealing with the uncertainty of intrinsically uncontrollable or difficult events'. Pfizer's organisational values are courage, excellence, equity, and joy. 'Courage' refers to the ability to think and act on a grand scale; 'excellence' is the commitment to consistently uphold high standards in the creation, production, and promotion of medicines; 'equity' involves creating equal and fair conditions for all stakeholders, particularly for patients in low-income countries; and 'joy' is the satisfaction and pride derived from one's work, along with the opportunity to improve people's lives (Pfizer, 2024).

**Food for thought:** ***How does a leader's personality influence the effective implementation of organisational strategy?***

**How it works in the pharmaceutical industry:** Description of Biocon's business and corporate strategies under Kiran Mazumdar-Shaw's leadership following its vision, mission, and organisational values (Appendix I).

## Corporate strategy (Where?)

Strategic decisions made by Kiran Mazumdar-Shaw have played a pivotal role in transforming Biocon from an industrial enzyme manufacturer into a leading player in the pharmaceutical and biopharmaceutical industries. In the mid-1990s, Mazumdar-Shaw reoriented Biocon towards the pharmaceutical market, focusing on two key areas: APIs and generics. During this period, the company concentrated on India and other developing countries, laying the groundwork for future expansion into new markets. Subsequently, Mazumdar-Shaw steered Biocon into the biopharmaceutical sector, achieving a significant milestone in 2001 when the company obtained FDA approval to produce lovastatin, enabling its entry into the US and European markets (Biocon, 2024a).

Under Mazumdar-Shaw's leadership, Biocon continues to expand its global presence across both regulated markets – evidenced by Biocon Biologics' acquisition of Viatris' biosimilars business in 2022 – and developing markets in Asia, Africa, and Latin America. The company now focuses on three core clusters: generics, biosimilars, and research services. Additionally, through sustained investment in R&D and strategic partnerships, Biocon is developing novel drugs, primarily targeting oncology and autoimmune diseases (Biocon, 2024b).

### Business strategy (How?)

In the 1990s, when Kiran Mazumdar-Shaw reoriented Biocon towards producing APIs and generics, the company adopted a cost leadership strategy. The focus was on the Indian market and other developing countries, where affordability was key (Biocon, 2024a). Biocon's strategic decision to enter the biosimilar market and focus on complex biologics such as insulin and monoclonal antibodies marked a shift in the company's business strategy. This transition led to the adoption of a hybrid approach combining cost leadership with differentiation. By entering regulated markets like the United States, Europe, and Japan, alongside developing markets, Biocon effectively employed a differentiation strategy to enhance its market presence.

Currently, under Kiran Mazumdar-Shaw's leadership, Biocon continues to leverage both cost leadership and differentiation business strategies, continually refining them through R&D innovations and the development of novel biosimilars. Additionally, its subsidiary, Syngene International Limited, offers differentiated R&D services to global clients, further bolstering Biocon's innovation capabilities. Implementing this hybrid business strategy has strengthened the company's competitive advantages and contributed to its sustainable development (Biocon, 2024b).

### Vision

Biocon's vision is effectively integrated with its business and corporate strategies, reflecting its primary focus for continuous efforts: 'To enhance global healthcare through innovative and affordable biopharmaceuticals for patients, partners, and healthcare systems across the globe' (Biocon, 2024b). Furthermore, under Mazumdar-Shaw's leadership, Biocon's vision extends beyond business objectives to encompass a strong social dimension. A core principle underpinning this vision is that healthcare innovations should serve as a tool for social progress and benefit humanity.

### Mission

Kiran Mazumdar-Shaw's philosophy closely aligns with Biocon's market positioning: 'We are a global biopharmaceutical company which believes that everyone has a right to affordable quality medicines'. Biocon defines its mission as 'to be an integrated biotechnology enterprise of global distinction' (Biocon, 2024b). This mission underscores a commitment to continuous innovation, the advancement of knowledge, adherence to quality systems, the development of human capital, and the fostering of mutually beneficial collaborations and partnerships. These principles guide the company's relationships with stakeholders, particularly with patients, focusing on delivering high-quality and affordable products and services.

### Organisational values

Biocon's organisational values directly reflect not only its stated vision and mission but also the leadership of Kiran Mazumdar-Shaw. Her strong commitment to innovation, accessibility, and social responsibility has transformed Biocon into a successful global enterprise. The core organisational values of Biocon include 'integrity and ethical behaviour', 'performance-driven work culture', 'value creation through innovation and differentiation', 'quality through compliance and best practices', and 'collaboration, teamwork and mutual respect' (Biocon, 2024b).

## 8.2 Constituents of organisational strategy

Leadership in the pharmaceutical industry depends on the successful implementation of strategy. An example of a strategy creation and implementation system is TASGRAM, which consists of seven components: thinking, analysing, strategy, goals, risks, actions, and monitoring (see Figure 8.2) (Aliekperov, 2021).

The leader and their team define ***thinking*** as the preliminary stage of strategy development, followed by analysis, coordination, and approval. Baldoni (2012, p. 125) noted that 'sound purpose begins with sound thinking – taking time to think before we do'. The effectiveness of this stage relies on the leader's systemic thinking skills and ability to view the system as a holistic picture consisting of interconnected elements.

At the ***analysing*** stage, the external and internal factors influencing the company's strategic development are thoroughly examined. According to Grant and Jordan (2015), successful strategy implementation depends on a profound understanding of the competitive environment and an objective appraisal of resources.

An industry attractiveness analysis can be conducted using tools such as PESTEL and Porter's Five Forces.

***PESTEL analysis*** is often employed to assess the feasibility of a company entering new markets. In the pharmaceutical industry, legal factors typically

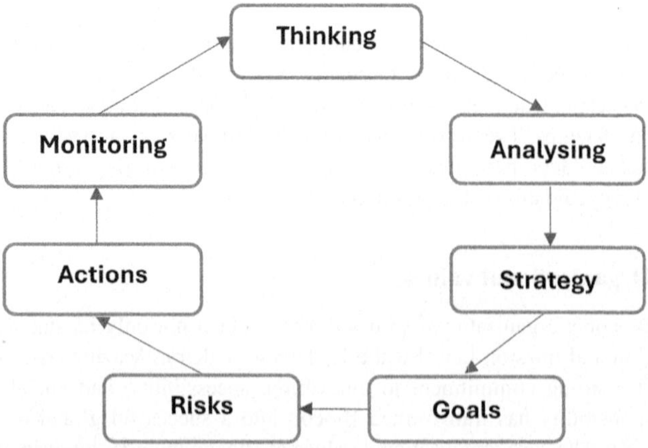


*Figure 8.2* Strategy creation and implementation system TASGRAM.

present the most significant challenges, as the sector is highly regulated. This includes licensing of premises, practices, and personnel; product registration; patent legislation; inspection of manufacturers and distributors; quality monitoring of drugs; and control of medical product promotion. Additionally, given the rapid advancement of digital technologies, technological factors are especially important industry development drivers.

***Porter's Five Forces analysis*** comprehensively assesses competitive forces that can significantly reduce an industry's attractiveness. The pharmaceutical sector is characterised by high entry barriers, especially when it comes to developing innovative drug therapies. However, a giant like Amazon has successfully entered the retail and wholesale markets of medicines, leveraging its resources and organisational capabilities (Nawrat, 2021).

***Stakeholder analysis, or the stakeholder matrix (power-interest grid)***, helps assess stakeholders' 'power' and 'interest'. In pharmaceutical companies, key stakeholders with high power and interest who should be managed closely include patients, doctors, employees, shareholders, and partners (such as academic centres, research laboratories, biotech companies, suppliers, and distributors). Legislative and regulatory authorities, as stakeholders with high power but low interest, should be kept satisfied. Competitors, who typically have low power and interest, need to be monitored. The community, with a high interest in ESG policy but relatively low power, should be kept informed.

To determine competitive advantages, a company should analyse its resources (tangible, intangible, and human) and organisational capabilities. A tool like ***VRIO (Valuable, Rare, Inimitable, and Organised) analysis*** can be used for this purpose. For companies such as Novartis, Gilead Sciences,

Pfizer, and Janssen Pharmaceutica, valuable and rare resources that are difficult to imitate include their brand, reputation, technology, patents, pharmaceutical products, ecosystems, and, of course, leaders like Daniel Vasella, John C. Martin, Paul Janssen, Albert Bourla, etc. In turn, competent managers ensure the efficient use of these resources, maintaining the organisation's successful and long-term development.

In addition to the tools mentioned above, others can be utilised, such as the 5W Client Analysis (a more detailed analysis of stakeholders such as clients), the BCG Matrix (for company portfolio analysis), and SWOT Analysis (for integrative analysis of internal and external environmental factors). The choice of analytical tools depends on the company's specifics, goals, organisational capabilities, and other relevant factors.

The ***strategy*** has been partially described in the previous sectioncovering corporate and business strategies.

Corporate strategy can be defined using the ***Ansoff Matrix***, which includes the following options: market penetration, product development, market development, and diversification. For example, Gilead Sciences, under the leadership of John C. Martin, focused on a product development strategy, creating unique antiviral drugs. WBA (n.d.) pursued a diversification strategy by entering new geographic markets and introducing new types of businesses, such as health services aimed at providing primary care, post-acute care, and home care.

Business strategy can be characterised using ***Porter's Generic Strategies analysis***, which includes the following elements: cost focus, differentiation focus, cost leadership, and differentiation. For example, Gilead Sciences employs a differentiation focus strategy by creating a unique value proposition for patients with HIV, hepatitis C, hepatitis B, and other viral diseases. Meanwhile, global companies like Pfizer, Merck, and Johnson & Johnson use a differentiation strategy, developing and producing medicines across various pharmacological groups, veterinary products, consumer goods, etc., which have competitive advantages due to their innovative characteristics, high quality, and customer experience. The cost leadership strategy is primarily characteristic of generic drug manufacturers, wholesale pharmaceutical companies, and pharmacy chains, which gain a competitive edge through more attractive pricing policies. Companies can also combine multiple business strategies, such as blending cost leadership with differentiation – for example, Biocon – to cater to specific market segments. This means that they can offer both competitive pricing and unique product features to different customer groups.

***Goals*** represent the desired state or outcome that an organisation aims to achieve. These goals should align with the organisation's mission, vision, and values and be directed towards implementing its strategy. Additionally, they should be constructed using the SMART criteria, meaning they should be specific, measurable, attainable, relevant, and timed. In Pfizer's case, the goal set by Albert Bourla at the onset of the COVID-19 pandemic was not just a goal but a reflection of Pfizer's vision, mission, values, and strategy (Fleischmann, 2022):

- ***Specific:*** Create an effective antiviral vaccine.
- ***Measurable:*** The vaccine's effectiveness had to meet the FDA requirements of at least 50%, but Pfizer set a higher minimum bar at 60%.
- ***Attainable:*** Despite the ambitious nature of the goal, Albert Bourla demonstrated persistence, allocating all necessary organisational resources and capabilities to achieve it.
- ***Relevant:*** Developing a COVID-19 vaccine aligned with Pfizer's strategy of innovative healthcare and integrating AI technologies into the company's operations.
- ***Timed:*** Dr. Bourla set a clear and ambitious timeline for his team: 'to develop a vaccine more quickly than anyone ever had before, ideally within six months' (Bourla, 2021).

***Risks*** are an integral part of the strategy implementation process. The thinking and analysing stages of the TASGRAM system help identify various types of organisational risks. For example, PESTEL analysis helps identify external risks; Porter's Five Forces analysis highlights competitive risks; and VRIO analysis reveals financial, operational, human, and other internal risks. SWOT analysis, as an effective integrative tool, comprehensively assesses both internal and external risks.

Depending on the magnitude (high/medium/low) and types of identified risks (strategic, operational, emerging, general), it is crucial to determine and implement appropriate management and response strategies. Companies can use the following approaches (Hopkin, 2013):

- ***Tolerate (low impact and likelihood):*** The risk is acceptable without taking additional measures.
- ***Treat (low impact and high likelihood):*** Measures are taken to manage the risks.
- ***Transfer (high impact and low likelihood):*** Use mechanisms such as insurance and hedging.
- ***Terminate (high impact and high likelihood):*** Cease or suspend the activities associated with the risk.

The next component of TASGRAM is ***actions.*** After defining the strategic directions for the organisation's development, setting desired goals, and assessing potential risks, it is crucial to implement strategic initiatives. For example, in line with Gilead Science's patient-oriented strategy, the goal was set to create a one-pill, once-daily HIV treatment to replace a cocktail of a dozen different drugs. To achieve this, John C. Martin and his team initiated a unique partnership with Bristol-Myers Squibb and Merck, which led to the creation of a combination drug under the Atripla brand, composed of three best-in-class HIV medications. As a result, HIV treatment was significantly simplified, patient compliance improved, and sustainable viral suppression was achieved (Yang et al., 2022).

***Monitoring*** involves assessing the effectiveness of strategy implementation. For pharmaceutical companies, key performance indicators include financial metrics (profits, revenue, expenses, and other financial outcomes), stakeholder satisfaction (doctors, patients, shareholders, communities, etc.), business processes (R&D, production, marketing, supply chain, etc.), and education & growth (innovations, products, technologies, personnel, etc.). Brand recognition and attractiveness are also critical metrics. Notably, Pfizer's 2022 revenues increased by 23% compared to 2021, exceeding $100 billion, with a significant 43% increase in reported net income. This substantial increase in net income bodes well for Pfizer's financial future. Dr Bourla stated, '2022 was a record-breaking year for Pfizer … in terms of the percentage of patients who have a positive perception of Pfizer and the work we do' (Pfizer, 2023b). He also noted a significant rise in employee engagement and commitment to organisational values. These achievements largely stem from improvements in various business processes; for example, in 2020, Pfizer achieved an industry-leading clinical success rate of 21%, maintained innovation quality, increased productivity, and continued to implement digital technologies across all business processes (Fernando et al., 2022). As a result, in 2022, the company ranked fourth among the World's Most Admired Companies, behind only Apple, Amazon, and Microsoft (Murray & Meyer, 2022).

**Food for thought: *Which constituents of an organisational strategy are shaped by the leader?***

**How it works in the pharmaceutical industry:** Description of the system for creating and implementing the TASGRAM strategy using the example of Novartis (Appendix E).

## Thinking

The creation of Novartis was preceded by extensive analytical work focused on gathering information, formulating a vision, and planning subsequent actions. The merger of two large pharmaceutical companies' resources and capabilities positioned Novartis to become a leader in the global pharmaceutical market. Daniel Vasella noted, 'I wanted to lead an organisation like Novartis because I believed it offered me the best opportunity to change people's lives for the better' (Bill George, 2015). After Daniel Vasella stepped down as CEO of Novartis, the strategy was adjusted, which also required a thorough preliminary analysis.

## Analysing

*External Environment* (Narasimhan, 2024):

*PESTEL Analysis:* For Novartis, it is crucial to monitor political developments and regulatory changes in the USA, Europe, Asia, Africa, Australasia, Canada, and Latin America. The company must anticipate technological changes and pay close attention to societal trends and environmental factors.

*Porter's Five Forces Analysis:* Novartis faces competition from both Big Pharma and smaller companies operating in regional and national markets.

*Stakeholder Analysis:* Daniel Vasella emphasised that patients' interests are more critical to the company than those of shareholders. Key stakeholders include employees, healthcare professionals, partner companies, government agencies, suppliers, investors, and communities.

*Internal Environment* (Narasimhan, 2024):

*VRIO Analysis:*

- *Valuable*: Novartis brand, innovation capabilities, relationships with partners, and ability to raise capital and attract investors.
- *Rare*: International presence, commercialisation experience, high adaptability, regulatory expertise, and ability to manage risks.
- *Inimitable:* Innovative products, technology platforms (including chemistry and biotherapeutics, cell therapy, gene therapy, radioligand therapy, and xRNA therapy), and CX.
- *Organisation:* Clear strategy, supportive organisational culture, leadership, professional management, and skilled employees.

## Strategy

Initially, Daniel Vasella built the company around a diversification strategy, bringing together patented pharmaceuticals, generic pharmaceuticals, vaccines and diagnostics, and consumer health under the Novartis brand. In 2015, the company shifted its strategy, positioning itself from a diversified healthcare group to a focused medicines company (Narasimhan, 2024).

*Corporate Strategy (Ansoff Matrix):*

- *Market Penetration:* Accelerating growth in priority geographies such as the United States, China, Germany, and Japan.
- *Product Development:* Strengthening core therapeutic areas, including cardiovascular-renal-metabolic, immunology, neuroscience, and oncology.

*Business Strategy (Porter's Generic Strategies Analysis):*

- *Differentiation:* Creating value for patients by developing innovative, high-quality drugs that improve quality of life and help people live longer.

## Goals

When creating Novartis, Daniel Vasella defined the company's primary goal as developing innovative therapies for treating rare and previously incurable diseases. At the same time, as a diversified company, Novartis also set goals for its other divisions. Currently, the company focuses solely on addressing unmet medical needs through innovative drug therapies.

Example of a SMART goal (Uhler & Brauner, 2022; Narasimhan, 2024):

- *Specific:* Launch the innovative drug Leqvio in the US market. Healthcare professionals administer it as a twice-yearly maintenance dose (priced at USD 3,250 per dose).
- *Measurable:* Obtain FDA approval (achieved in 2021), secure prescriptions from cardiologists, and meet planned targets for profit, revenue, expenses, reimbursement, and pharmacovigilance.
- *Attainable:* Create an ecosystem to increase the drug's availability to patients (e.g., specialty pharmacies, patient and healthcare professional support programmes, education, and overcoming clinical barriers).
- *Relevant:* Align with corporate strategy (priority market – USA/ core therapeutic area – cardiovascular) and business strategy (unique, innovative therapy that improves the quality of life).
- *Timed:* The expected US level of effort is planned for the long term (through 2036+).

## Risks

Creating innovative drugs, especially for rare diseases, is always associated with risks, so Daniel Vasella had to discuss and address potential risks with shareholders.

Currently, Novartis manages various types of risks in the following areas (Novartis, 2023a):

- *Strategic:* Key products and commercial priorities; R&D; pricing, reimbursement, and access; alliances, acquisitions, and divestments; intellectual property, etc.
- *Operational:* Cybersecurity and data protection; implementation of strategic technology programmes; talent management; legal, regulatory, ethics, and compliance; manufacturing and product quality, etc.
- *Emerging:* Geopolitical developments; macroeconomic changes; climate change; tax laws and developments, etc.
- *General:* Indebtedness; foreign currency exchange rates; key customers; pension plans, etc.

## Actions

To ensure Novartis's sustainable development, Daniel Vasella decided to create the Novartis R&D Center, which shaped the company's subsequent transition to translational medicine (Armstrong, 2009).

Bringing an innovative drug like Leqvio to the US market involves complex, interrelated actions that align with the planned goals and approved strategy. These actions include (Uhler & Brauner, 2022):

- Providing the necessary results from laboratory, animal, and human clinical testing to obtain FDA approval.
- Implementing subsequent testing, manufacturing, and commercialisation of Leqvio for the US market.
- Ensuring drug availability by partnering with large health systems focused on heart disease and cardiologists; including Leqvio, in reimbursement programmes; ensuring proper administration conditions in specialty pharmacies; and implementing supportive programmes for patients and healthcare professionals.

## Monitoring

The diversification strategy, focusing on creating value for patients with rare and incurable diseases, has borne fruit: Novartis has become one of the fastest-growing companies in the industry.

Novartis' strategy, centred on innovative medicines, consistently drives annual sales growth. In 2023, financial indicators highlighted the effectiveness of this strategy: net sales (revenues) grew by 8%, and net income (profit) increased by 42% (Novartis, 2023a). Novartis also aims to become a global leader in material ESG factors. Therefore, it sets high-performance indicators for innovations, product quality and patient safety, supply chain, environmental impact, employee well-being, access to healthcare, animal welfare, political engagement, and ethical business practices (Novartis, 2023b).

## 8.3 Essence, types, and stages of organisational changes

The successful long-term development of an organisation depends on the leader's ability and willingness to implement effective organisational changes amidst uncertainty and discontinuity. Drucker noted that only organisations capable of change survive in times of turbulence (Drucker & Maciariello, 2012).

Some leadership theories also emphasise that a leader must be an agent of change. According to Bass's transformational leadership theory, a leader serves as a role model who inspires others to go the 'extra mile' and achieve results that exceed expectations (Bass, 1985). Heifetz's adaptive leadership theory suggests that a leader focuses on the adaptations required of people in response to changing environments (Heifetz & Laurie, 2001).

Initiating and leading the change process is what distinguishes a leader from a manager. A leader challenges the status quo, whereas a manager accepts the status quo; a leader keeps their eye on the horizon, while a manager keeps their eye on the bottom line; a leader does the right things, while a manager does things right (Kotter, 1990). Kotter (2001) characterised the differences between a leader and a manager in this way: 'They [leaders] don't make plans; they don't solve problems; they don't even organise people. What leaders really do is prepare organisations for change and help them cope as they struggle through it'.

According to Nadler and Tushman (1980), organisational change can be viewed in terms of the following two dimensions:

- Incremental & strategic
- Reactive & anticipatory

***Incremental changes*** affect individual functional processes or components within an organisation, such as the organisational structure, the implementation of new technologies, and changes in the functioning of specific departments (R&D, production, logistics, marketing, etc.). These changes are typical for almost all organisations, and their main goal is to improve the organisation's efficiency in line with the approved strategy for its development. Although incremental changes should remain under the monitoring of the organisation's leader, they are primarily the responsibility of managers.

***Strategic changes*** in an organisation, such as its basic structures, systems, processes, mission, vision, and organisational values, are initiated by the leader. Their success is not solely dependent on the leader's will and persistence but also on the presence of a professional and motivated team. Equally important is a clear, well-thought-out organisational strategy which guides the implementation of these changes. A prime example is Charles Walgreen III, who, with an inspiring vision and strategy and a strong team, transformed the family company into a leader in the US pharmacy chain market.

***Reactive changes***, which often arise from urgent and unfavourable circumstances, can impact both individual functional units and the organisation as a whole. Albert Bourla and his team swiftly and effectively responded to the urgency of the challenges posed by the COVID-19 pandemic, significantly bolstering Pfizer's leadership position in the industry.

***Anticipatory changes*** are carried out in a gradual and planned manner to improve organisational indicators. Such changes allow the company to develop sustainably and adapt to the business environment. Thus, Vasella initiated a gradual reorientation of Novartis from the creation of chemical compounds to biological drugs in 2002, moving the global R&D headquarters from Basel to Cambridge and hiring a leading cardiologist from Harvard as its head (Armstrong, 2009).

The combination of these dimensions forms the following four types of organisational changes (Nadler & Tushman, 1980):

- Tuning (anticipatory/incremental)
- Adaptation (reactive/incremental)
- Re-orientation (anticipatory/strategic)
- Re-creation (reactive/strategic)

***Tuning*** is a partial, consistent change that involves modifying individual structural components of a company to improve operational efficiency and enhance innovative capabilities. For example, tuning may include opening new production capacities, optimising supply chain management, implementing new digital technologies to improve the R&D process, quality management, CX, and more.

***Adaptation*** refers to partial changes in response to unforeseen shifts in the external environment. This may include adjustments to the procedures for conducting preclinical or clinical trials due to updated regulatory requirements, changes in the supply chain due to political or economic threats, modifications to the quality assurance system in response to emerging risks from low-quality raw materials, or revisions to pricing and promotion strategies in reaction to competitors' actions. The response of pharmaceutical companies to the COVID-19 pandemic is a clear example of adaptation. For instance, the Walgreens pharmacy chain, along with other leading American pharmacy chains, quickly provided drive-through COVID-19 testing at its locations, optimised customer communications through digital tools, and established cooperation with other stakeholders in the healthcare system (Knox, 2021).

***Re-orientation*** is a consistent structural change within an organisation that impacts its strategy, culture, structure, and other components of organisational design. The advantage of re-orientation lies in its ability to implement changes thoughtfully and gradually, allowing leaders ample time to build coalitions, delegate authority to key managers, prepare personnel for upcoming changes, and minimise potential risks. For example, since 2015, Novartis has been re-orienting itself from a diversified healthcare group to a focused medicines company. The company has exited the animal health, vaccines, and consumer health markets as part of this strategy (Novartis, 2023a).

***Re-creation*** is an organisational change associated with the most significant risks, typically involving structural and complex transformations during a deep organisational crisis and within a limited time frame. New leaders often initiate these organisational changes, impacting core organisational values. For example, the global pharmaceutical company Valeant Pharmaceuticals International, Inc. faced a deep crisis due to massive debt, accounting violations, and unethical management practices. Joseph C. Papa, who became the company's new CEO in 2016, implemented a comprehensive restructuring to reduce debt, revise the product portfolio, and stabilise pricing policies. The company was also rebranded, reflected in the name change to Bausch Health Companies Inc., along with a transformation of its organisational culture to emphasise customer focus, innovation, and building trusting relationships with partners (Thomas, 2018).

It is worth noting that organisational changes such as tuning and adaptation are typically the responsibility of managers, as these changes are implemented in alignment with the existing organisational strategy. The leader's role is primarily to oversee the process, inspire the team, and help secure necessary resources. On the other hand, strategic transformations – re-orientation and re-creation – demand an exceptional leadership approach, as they directly involve altering the systems and processes that managers oversee.

According to Kotter (1995), there are eight stages in implementing strategic changes in an organisation:

| | |
|---|---|
| Step 1 – Establish a sense of urgency. | Step 5 – Remove obstacles. |
| Step 2 – Build a large, powerful coalition. | Step 6 – Generate short-term wins. |
| Step 3 – Develop a vision for change. | Step 7 – Build on wins. |
| Step 4 – Communicate the vision. | Step 8 – Embed changes into culture. |

The first step – ***establishing a sense of urgency*** – begins when the leader recognises the inevitability of organisational changes. This realisation typically results from analysing trends and drivers, assessing the current situation within the company, identifying external threats, and more. This step reflects on the components of the TASGRAM system, such as thinking and analysing. Open communication and discussions about potential opportunities and risks are essential at this stage. The leader must gain the support of employees, as Kotter (1995) suggests that success is more likely if about 75% of managers share and understand the importance of organisational changes.

The second step – ***building a large, powerful coalition*** – focuses on involving as many people as possible in the organisational change process, leveraging the leader's ability to inspire, unite, and persuade others. It is essential to distinguish between a 'leader's team' and a 'coalition'. A team typically consists of no more than 8–10 people, while a coalition can be much broader.

The third step – ***developing a vision for change*** – aims to create a clear and compelling 'picture of the future' for key stakeholders, including shareholders, employees, partners, and clients. As Kotter (1995) noted, 'If you can't communicate the vision to someone in five minutes or less and get a reaction that signifies both understanding and interest, you are not done'. This vision, along with the organisation's development strategy, is essential, as without it, the team's efforts risk becoming uncoordinated, chaotic, and ineffective.

The fourth stage – ***communicating the vision*** – requires the leader and their team to convey information about the vision, strategy, and upcoming changes to all stakeholders. A variety of communication tools, both online and offline, should be employed for this purpose. Additionally, involving employees, including those at lower levels, is crucial in refining certain aspects of the strategic alternatives. This approach can significantly motivate employees, as they will see their personal contribution to the strategic management decisions that are vital to the organisation.

The fifth stage – ***removing obstacles*** – involves empowering employees to engage them effectively in organisational change. One common obstacle at this stage is an overly bureaucratic organisational structure. Additionally, challenges may arise from individual employees who hold authority and power within the organisation but resist change. Therefore, the leader must ensure that their team comprises individuals who share their values and understand the need for change.

The sixth stage – ***generating short-term wins*** – aims to maintain the motivation and morale of employees during the implementation of organisational changes. Downplaying the importance of small victories can diminish the enthusiasm and involvement of personnel. The leader should focus on short-term achievements, such as increasing market share, creating an innovative medical product, improving reputation, and rewarding the people involved in these processes. It is important to remember that achieving initial successes significantly increases trust in the leader, reassures the team, and inspires further achievements.

The seventh step – ***building on wins*** – involves further transforming functional processes, structures, and systems according to the leader's vision. At this stage, it is important to 'feed' the organisation with new people who stimulate further development, reward and promote employees who have contributed most significantly to implementing the transformational vision, and initiate new projects. According to Kotter (1995), the main mistakes at this stage include celebrating achievements too early and decreasing the organisation's development pace.

The eighth and final stage – ***embedding changes into culture*** – ensures that new transformational approaches are fully integrated into the organisational culture. To achieve this, it is essential to demonstrate the benefits of behaviours aligned with organisational values, emphasise successfully achieved goals, maintain a high level of communication, and more. The formation of deep values is a long-term process; the new organisational worldview should be gradually introduced into the company's structure, policies, and functional processes.

For the organisation to thrive, it is essential to train new leaders who will embody the organisational culture. According to Kotter (1995), making a mistake in choosing a leader's successor can be very costly for the organisation, potentially undermining its previous achievements. It is important to remember that only in an organisation where an atmosphere of trust and openness is maintained can a system be formed that promotes the development of new leaders.

**Food for thought:** ***What actions should a leader take to address challenges at each stage of transformation?***

**How it works in the pharmaceutical industry:** Description of Kotter's eight stages of implementing strategic changes using the example of Pfizer under Albert Bourla's leadership (see Appendix D).

## Step 1 – Establish a sense of urgency

The need for digital transformation of the business was driven by Albert Bourla's desire to make the company more cost-effective and more focused on science and patients. Introducing digital technologies at every stage in the value chain would help achieve these results. The success of digitalisation in the company's activities was measured by achieving an ambitious goal – 25 breakthrough drugs by 2025 (Bio-IT World, 2021). Dr Bourla demonstrated his commitment to Pfizer's digital transformation by introducing a new position, CDO, on the day of his appointment as CEO in January 2019. The CDO was given the first task – digitalising the drug discovery and development process. This marked the beginning of Pfizer's strategic transformation into a digitalised company (Cardoso, 2021).

### Step 2 – Build a large, powerful coalition

Despite creating a team led by the CDO, it was necessary to scale new ways of working and involve many people in this process. The transformation affected all key functional areas in the organisation: R&D, production, logistics, marketing and sales, and interaction with stakeholders (doctors, patients, regulatory authorities). Using digital tools increased the accuracy and speed of decision-making at all organisational levels. The COVID-19 pandemic significantly accelerated digitalisation, partly due to Bourla's goal for his employees – to create an antiviral vaccine within a few months. It also allowed Bourla to expand the coalition of employees directly involved in using technologies such as AI and ML. This motivated people and enabled them to see the benefits of Pfizer's digital transformation (Bio-IT World, 2021).

### Step 3 – Develop a vision for change

Pfizer's digital transformation is grounded in the company's mission – 'Breakthroughs that change patients' lives' (Pfizer, 2024) – which led to the definition of three strategic priorities for Pfizer Digital (Pfizer, 2023c):

- Improve patient outcomes
- Deliver medicines to patients faster
- Drive the revolutionary treatments of tomorrow

As Lydia Fonseca, Pfizer's CDO, noted, 'It's not about creating a digital strategy for our business but about creating a business strategy for a digital world' (Buntz, 2023).

### Step 4 – Communicate the vision

To convince people of the need for digital transformation at Pfizer, it was essential to share a clear vision of the future with them: What does it look like? Why is change necessary? How will it benefit the company, employees, and other stakeholders? Additionally, it was crucial to support people throughout the process, gather their feedback, and involve them in subsequent stages of the transformational transition. At Pfizer, a mini roadshow was introduced to present the vision of the digital future to those hesitant about change. Employees who supported the transformation were encouraged to participate in Agile sprint retrospectives and work sessions to develop and share ideas for new projects. They also had the opportunity to join various programmes, enabling them to contribute to Pfizer's digital transformation (Bio-IT World, 2021).

## Step 5 – Remove obstacles

In addition to making decisions to reduce people's resistance to change during the transition to a digital business model, training them in new knowledge and skills was necessary. This approach not only removed obstacles but also scaled new ways of working and transformed the organisation's training and talent development methods. Pfizer began to adopt 'horizontal' thinking, focusing on the patient experience rather than its own 'vertical' functional processes. The company prioritised achieving results by implementing flexible, cross-functional ways of working. Optimising the organisational structure and introducing new working methods allowed Pfizer to minimise bureaucracy and create a more flexible and adaptive company (Olavsrud, 2022).

## Step 6 – Generate short-term wins

The most significant achievement at Pfizer, which not only demonstrated the strategic benefits of digitalisation but also significantly accelerated the digital transformation process, was the development of a vaccine against COVID-19. Thanks to investments in digital tools, the vaccine was developed in just 269 days instead of the usual 8–10 years, exemplifying what Lydia Fonseca referred to as the 'speed of light' concept (Buntz, 2023).

Key factors contributing to this success included (Bio-IT World, 2021; Buntz, 2023):

- The scientific data cloud, created in 2019 in partnership with AWS, enabled faster analysis and computational research to identify and develop new molecules.
- Virtual monitoring allowed the clinical trial to expand to 46,000 participants across 150 sites in six countries.

- COVID-19 incidence prediction models optimised the selection of clinical trial locations.
- AI and ML assisted in quality checking and analysing vast volumes of trial data in near real-time.
- Augmented reality (AR) technologies facilitated the diagnostics, maintenance, and repair of lab and manufacturing equipment.
- Real-time digital monitoring of supplies and temperatures worldwide optimised vaccine transportation.
- An entirely virtual submission of the application for FDA approval of the vaccine enabled the reduction of bureaucratic obstacles.
- Albert Bourla emphasised that the joy and pride felt by Pfizer employees stemmed not only from developing the vaccine but also from being part of a company that is solving global challenges (Gurchiek, 2021).

### Step 7 – Build on wins

The success of the COVID-19 vaccine development has further catalysed Pfizer's digital transformation. For example, in 2021, the company significantly increased its investment in cloud technologies, migrating 12,000 applications and 8,000 servers to the cloud within 42 weeks. This move also saved the company $47 million annually and reduced $CO_2$ emissions. Additionally, Pfizer invested in supercomputing capabilities, which reduced the time required for calculations and scientific simulations by 80–90% (Buntz, 2023). These advancements necessitated further employee engagement, fostering a solid commitment to the company's digital transformation. Moreover, attracting new talent who share Pfizer's values and core purpose – 'Breakthroughs that change patients' lives' – has accelerated and strengthened digital transformation outcomes.

### Step 8 – Embed changes into culture

To embed the digital development model into Pfizer's organisational culture, it is essential to continually create new opportunities to engage people and develop their talents. For example, Pfizer's Global Center for Digital Innovation (CDI) was established to generate breakthrough ideas aimed at improving health and enhancing the quality of customer service in line with the strategic priorities of Pfizer Digital (Pfizer, 2023c). Creating a digital ecosystem within the healthcare system also plays a crucial role in the success of the transformation process. As Lydia Fonseca noted, 'Transformations succeed only when the whole organisation becomes the change you're trying to achieve' (Chadha, 2022).

## 8.4 Conclusions

1 The company's development vision is realised through a strategy developed by its leader and team. The strategy can be viewed from two perspectives: (1) defining the company's market positioning to differentiate it from competitors and (2) creating customer value. To achieve this, companies utilise corporate strategy (where) and business strategy (how). The effective integration of these approaches contributes to the company's sustainable development in alignment with its vision, mission, and values.
2 The TASGRAM model can be utilised to create and implement a strategy. It consists of interconnected constituents: thinking, analysing, strategy, goals, risks, actions, and monitoring. Thinking involves defining a preliminary strategy, while analysing focuses on studying the internal and external environment. This is followed by formulating corporate and business strategies, setting strategic goals, identifying and managing risks, and implementing the strategy through agreed actions. The final stage is monitoring the success of the strategy using specific indicators.
3 For the organisation's successful transformation, the leader must act as an agent of change, focusing primarily on strategic organisational transformations such as reorientation and recreation while also monitoring incremental changes like tuning and adaptation. Organisational change management is a complex and systematic process that involves not only changes in strategy, systems, and processes but also reducing resistance to change, fostering commitment to the new development model, attracting new talent, and more.

## References

Aliekperov, A., (2021). *Creating Business and Corporate Strategy: An Integrated Strategic System*. London: Routledge.

Armstrong, W., (2009). The Book on Daniel. *Pharmaceutical Executive* [online], 01 October 2009. Available from: https://www.pharmexec.com/view/book-daniel [Accessed 22 February 2024].

Baldoni, J., (2012). *Lead with Purpose: Giving Your Organization a Reason to Believe in Itself.* New York: AMACOM.

Bass, B.M., (1985). *Leadership and Performance Beyond Expectations*. New York: Free Press.

Bill George, (2015). Daniel Vasella: The long journey toward leadership. *Bill George* [online], 13 July 2015. Available from: https://billgeorge.org/blog/daniel-vasella-the-long-journey-toward-leadership/ [Accessed 10 May 2024].

Biocon, (2024a). *Our legacy. Biocon [online]*. Available from: https://www.biocon.com/about-us/our-legacy/ [Accessed 10 December 2024].

Biocon, (2024b). *Who we are. Biocon [online]*. Available from: https://www.biocon.com/about-us/who-we-are/ [Accessed 10 December 2024].

Bio-IT World, (2021). Pfizer's digital strategy and transformation. *Bio-IT World* [online]. Available from: https://www.bio-itworld.com/news/2021/07/20/pfizer-s-digital-strategy-and-transformation [Accessed 12 July 2024].

Bourla, A., (2021). The CEO of Pfizer on developing a vaccine in record time. *Harvard Business Review* [online], May. Available from: https://hbr.org/2021/05/the-ceo-of-pfizer-on-developing-a-vaccine-in-record-time [Accessed 07 February 2024].

Buntz, B., (2023). Pfizer exec frames digital as a core business strategy. *Drug Discovery Trends* [online], 06 December 2023. Available from: https://www.drugdiscovery trends.com/pfizer-exec-frames-digital-as-a-core-business-strategy/ [Accessed 24 July 2024].

Cardoso, J., (2021). Without digital we wouldn't be here even today – Albert Bourla, Pfizer CEO. *Medium* [online], 15 March 2021. Available from: https://joaquimcar dosodorosario.medium.com/without-digital-we-wouldnt-be-here-even-today-albert-bourla-pfizer-ceo-f6f3daf4b9f3 [Accessed 05 July 2024].

Chadha, S., (2022). How digital helps a life sciences leader move at light speed. *McKinsey & Company* [online], 31 May 2022. Available from: https://www.mckinsey.com/industries/life-sciences/our-insights/how-digital-helps-a-life-sciences-leader-move-at-light-speed [Accessed 24 July 2024].

Collins, J., (2001). *Good to Great*. London: Random House Business Books.

Drucker, P., & Maciariello, J., (2012). *The daily Drucker: 366 days of insight and motivation for getting the right things done*. New York: HarperBusiness.

Fernando, K., Menon, S., Jansen, K., Naik, P., Nucci, G., Roberts, J., Wu, S.S., & Dolsten, M., (2022). Achieving end-to-end success in the clinic: Pfizer's learnings on R&D productivity. *Drug Discovery Today*, 27(3), 697–704. https://doi.org/10.1016/j.drudis.2021.12.010

Fleischmann, A., (2022). Albert Bourla. Chairman and CEO, Pfizer. *Leadership Matters* [online], 05 April 2022. Available from: https://www.leadershipmattersshow.com/episodes/albert-bourla [Accessed 15 February 2024].

Gilead, (2022). *Gilead Sciences to Acquire Pharmasset, Inc. for $11 Billion* [online], Gilead Sciences, Inc. Available from: https://www.gilead.com/news-and-press/press-room/press-releases/2011/11/gilead-sciences-to-acquire-pharmasset-inc-for-11-billion [Accessed 01 March 2024].

Grant, R.M., & Jordan, J.J., (2015). *Foundations of Strategy*. 2nd edition. Hoboken, New Jersey: John Wiley & Sons.

Gurchiek, K., (2021). Pfizer and SHRM CEOs discuss COVID-19, value of culture. *SHRM* [online], 17 March 2021. Available from: https://www.shrm.org/topics-tools/news/pfizer-shrm-ceos-discuss-covid-19-value-culture [Accessed 16 February 2024].

Heifetz, R.A., & Laurie, D.L., (2001). The work of leadership. *Harvard Business Review* [online], December. Available from: https://hbr.org/2001/12/the-work-of-leadership [Accessed 26 May 2024].

Hopkin, P., (2013). *Risk Management*. London: Kogan Page Publishers.

Knox, D., (2021). How Walgreens Boots Alliance is embracing an entrepreneurial mindset. *Forbes* [online], 8 April 2021. Available from: https://www.forbes.com/sites/daveknox/2021/04/08/how-walgreens-boots-alliance-is-embracing-an-entre preneurial-mindset/ [Accessed 05 February 2024].

Kotter, J.P., (1990). *Force for Change: How Leadership Differs from Management*. New York: The Free Press.

Kotter, J.P., (1995). Leading change: Why transformation efforts fail. *Harvard Business Review* [online], May–June 1995. Available from: https://hbr.org/1995/05/leading-change-why-transformation-efforts-fail-2 [Accessed 12 June 2024].

Kotter, J.P., (2001). What leaders really do. *Harvard Business Review* [online], December. Available from: https://hbr.org/2001/12/what-leaders-really-do?ab=at_art_art_1x4_s01 [Accessed 3 June 2024].

Murray, A., & Meyer, D., (2022). Pfizer, Apple, Microsoft, Amazon among world's most admired companies. *Fortune* [online], 02 February 2022. Available from: https://fortune.com/2022/02/02/pfizer-apple-microsoft-amazon-worlds-most-admired-companies-ceo-daily/ [Accessed 02 May 2024].

Nadler, D., & Tushman, M., (1980). A model for diagnosing organizational behavior. *Organizational Dynamics*, 9(2), 35–51.

Narasimhan, V., (2024). Novartis strategy and growth update. *J.P. Morgan Healthcare Conference* [online]. Available from: https://www.novartis.com/sites/novartis_com/files/2024-jpm-novartis-strategy-growth-update.pdf [Accessed 05 March 2025].

Nawrat, A., (2021). Enter Amazon Pharmacy: The beginning of a great online pharmacy fight? *Pharmaceutical Technology* [online], 18 January 2021. Available from: https://www.pharmaceutical-technology.com/features/amazon-pharmacy-disruption-healthcare/?cf-view [Accessed 09 March 2024].

Novartis, (2023a). *Novartis annual report 2023*. Available at: https://www.novartis.com/de-de/sites/novartis_de/files/novartis-annual-report-2023.pdf [Accessed 22 May 2024].

Novartis, (2023b). *Novartis in society: Reporting criteria 2023*. Available from: https://www.novartis.com/sites/novartis_com/files/novartis-in-society-reporting-criteria-2023.pdf [Accessed 22 May 2024].

Olavsrud, T., (2022). Pfizer drives digital operations overhaul. *CIO* [online], 10 August 2021. Available from: https://www.cio.com/article/189094/pfizer-drives-digital-operations-overhaul.html [Accessed 14 July 2024].

Pfizer, (2023a). *Pfizer Sets New Ambition: Changing a Billion Lives a Year by 2027* [online], Pfizer. Available from: https://www.pfizer.com/news/announcements/pfizer-sets-new-ambition-changing-billion-lives-year-2027 [Accessed 06 March 2024].

Pfizer, (2023b). A record-breaking year and strong fourth quarter for Pfizer. Pfizer [online]. Available from: https://insights.pfizer.com/fourth-quarter-fy-earnings/ [Accessed 01 March 2024].

Pfizer, (2023c). *Center for digital innovation. Pfizer [online]*. Available from: https://centerfordigitalinnovation.pfizer.com/ [Accessed 11 July 2024].

Pfizer, (2024). *Our Purpose* [online], Pfizer Inc. Available from: https://www.pfizer.com/about/purpose [Accessed 06 March 2024].

Porter, M.E., (1985). *Competitive Advantage*. New York: Free Press.

Ratcliffe, S., (2016). 'Joel Arthur Barker'. Oxford Essential Quotations. *Oxford University Press* [online]. Available from: https://www.oxfordreference.com/display/10.1093/acref/9780191826719.001.0001/q-oro-ed4-00011987 [Accessed 25 May 2024].

Schein, E.H., & Schein, P.A., (2017). *Organisational Culture and Leadership*. 5th edition. San Francisco: Wiley & Sons.

Thomas, K., (2018). Valeant to shed its tarnished name and rebrand as Bausch Health. *The New York Times* [online], 08 May 2018. Available from: https://www.nytimes.com/2018/05/08/health/valeant-name-bausch-drugs.html [Accessed 20 June 2024].

Uhler, T., & Brauner, J., (2022). An innovative sales strategy for a pivotal drug: Leqvio, *Recon Strategy* [online], 19 August 2022. Available from: https://reconstrategy.com/2022/08/an-innovative-sales-strategy-for-a-pivotal-drug-leqvio/#:~:text=Following%20FDA%20approval%20of%20Leqvio,instead%20of%20primarily%20targeting%20physicians [Accessed 20 May 2024].

WBA, (n.d.). *Living our purpose, vision and values. Walgreens Boots Alliance [online]*. Available from: https://www.walgreensbootsalliance.com/about-us/living-our-purpose-vision-and-values [Accessed 07 March 2024].

Welch, J., & Welch, S., (2005). *Winning*. New York: Harper Business.healthcare.

Yang, T., Oliyai, R., & Kent, K.M., (2022). The making of the one pill – Developing single tablet regimens for HIV and for HCV. *Antiviral Therapy*, 27(2). https://doi.org/10.1177/13596535211067606

# Concluding remark

Although leadership still remains an open book, continuously adapted and supplemented in response to various political, economic, and social factors, leaders' role and impact remain pivotal in organisations' development. The pharmaceutical industry, as one of the most critical sectors for ensuring people's quality of life, in addition to universal approaches to leadership, is also characterised by a significant need to adhere to moral and ethical principles, particularly in the development of innovative pharmaceutical products.

In this book, leadership issues in the pharmaceutical industry are consistently explored, *integrating leadership theories with practical examples of leaders* who have significantly contributed to creating innovative drug therapies and providing effective and affordable medicines to patients, including those in impoverished and remote regions worldwide.

The book '*Leadership in the Pharmaceutical Industry: From Theory to Practice*' focuses on leadership in pharmaceutical organisations at three levels: *individual*, *team*, and *organisational*. At the *individual level*, the characteristics of leadership, fundamental leadership theories, types of leaders, differences between leadership and management, and leadership traits and skills are examined. Subsequently, the implementation of leadership at the *team level* is discussed, focusing on various leadership styles, approaches to team interaction, and both extrinsic and intrinsic motivational factors.

At the *organisational level*, leadership is analysed in the context of organisational culture, strategy, and change management. Additionally, the ethics of a leader's behaviour in the pharmaceutical industry, including examples of unethical and destructive leadership, as well as the types of innovations typical of the pharmaceutical business, are examined.

It is worth noting that special attention should now be given to the *digital transformation* of the pharmaceutical industry, which is a key responsibility of contemporary leaders. The influence of the Fourth Industrial Revolution – encompassing technological innovations such as AI, ML, big data, cloud

DOI: 10.4324/9781003617266-10

computing, and virtual and augmented reality – profoundly impacts the value chain of pharmaceutical organisations, particularly in the development of innovative therapies for rare and previously incurable diseases. The integrative utilisation of digital technologies is becoming an inevitable feature of modern leadership. This includes the development of new skills, fostering team collaboration, shaping organisational culture and strategy, and addressing other aspects of leadership in the pharmaceutical industry. Ultimately, all these efforts must be directed towards achieving and maintaining a high standard of well-being and quality of life for people worldwide.

# Appendices

## Appendix A: Biography of Paul Janssen

Paul Janssen was born in 1926 in Belgium. His father was a doctor who founded a small pharmaceutical company in 1934. Firstly, Janssen studied medicine at the Catholic University of Leuven before graduating with honours from the University of Ghent in 1951. The young scientist also developed an interest in pharmacology. In 1956, he earned a doctorate in pharmacology from Ghent while working part-time as an assistant to Nobel Prize winner Corneille Heymans. He also studied at the Institute of Pharmacology at the University of Cologne. Even then, Paul Janssen aspired to create new drugs by synthesising various chemical components, and he began to realise this dream in a laboratory equipped in his father's garage.

In 1953, Paul founded Janssen Pharmaceutica, which focused on developing and testing new chemical compounds. Within three years, approximately 800 compounds were synthesised, eight of which entered the market as drugs. The new company, dedicated exclusively to research and development, succeeded by selling licences for its inventions to pharmaceutical companies. In 1961, the world-renowned Johnson & Johnson acquired Janssen Pharmaceutica, and Paul was appointed director of research, granting him broad powers (Lewi & Smith, 2007; Gurowitz, 2015).

Over nearly 40 years, Janssen and his team developed 79 original drugs, including neuroleptics, analgesics, antifungal, antiparasitic, gastrointestinal, and cardiovascular medications. Among the most famous are Haldol, Ergamisol, Vermox, Daktarin, Priamide, Nemicide, Dipidolor, and others. Paul Janssen's laboratory also made significant contributions to the fields of pharmacology, biochemistry, toxicology, statistics, and more, publishing up to 200 scientific papers annually. In 1991, Paul stepped down as research director and founded the Centre for Molecular Design, where virtual modelling of chemical components was conducted, primarily for developing medicines to treat HIV (Lewi & Smith, 2007).

Dr Janssen noted that there are two key criteria for conducting effective research: competent and highly motivated people and continuous critical analysis. He saw his leadership role as an orchestra conductor, coordinating the work of diverse, highly qualified specialists – chemists, pharmacologists, toxicologists, clinicians, and statisticians – to achieve a common goal. He understood that strict regulation of processes would not yield positive results, as many discoveries happen unplanned, distinguishing the nature of a scientific laboratory from that of production or sales. Dr Janssen gave his employees considerable freedom, fostering their desire to acquire new knowledge while maintaining high-performance expectations. The laboratory staff addressed Paul Janssen as Dr Paul, reflecting their respect and commitment (Lewi & Smith, 2007).

During his lifetime, Dr Janssen received numerous awards, including five honorary professorships and 22 honorary doctorates, making him one of the most prolific researchers in the field of new drug development. Paul Janssen held over 100 patents and was the author or co-author of over 850 scientific publications. Paul Janssen was a man of many talents: he played the piano, excelled at chess, had a phenomenal memory, and was deeply fascinated by history. He was also uniquely able to visualise and design molecular structures when developing new chemical compounds (Gurowitz, 2015).

In 2003, Dr Janssen passed away at 77 while attending a conference in Rome, Italy. In his memory, the Dr Paul Janssen Award for Biomedical Research has been awarded annually since 2004 to scientists who have significantly advanced human health (Johnson & Johnson, n.d.).

## Appendix B: Biography of John C. Martin

John C. Martin was born into a family of chemists in 1951 in Easton, Pennsylvania. He earned a Bachelor of Science in Chemical Engineering from Purdue University in 1973, followed by a PhD in Organic Chemistry from the University of Chicago in 1977. In 1984, he also obtained an MBA in marketing from Golden Gate University in San Francisco. John Martin began his professional career as a laboratory researcher. He later joined Syntex Corp., where he worked from 1978 to 1984 as a researcher and then as a research team leader. A significant breakthrough for John C. Martin and his team was the development of Cytovene, a drug used to treat viral eye infections, particularly in patients with HIV. From 1984 to 1990, he served as the director of antiviral chemistry at Bristol-Myers Squibb (Lou et al., 2022).

Martin experienced a pivotal moment early in his professional career. In 1988, at a scientific conference on the Chemotherapy of AIDS in Oxnard, California, he had the opportunity to speak with Paul Janssen. The legendary scientist asked the young researcher about his goals and plans. John C. Martin said he would like to become as successful a leader in creating innovative drugs as his interlocutor. Paul Janssen replied, 'I give you one chance out of one hundred'. John C. Martin smiled and responded, 'That is enough.

I will take that chance'. It is worth noting that John C. Martin seized that opportunity and became a successful leader in drug development (Li & De Clercq, 2022).

In 1990, he joined Gilead Sciences as Vice President of Research and Development. Under his leadership, the company developed and launched three effective antiviral drugs for the treatment of AIDS and hepatitis B, which brought significant commercial success. In 1996, Martin became CEO of Gilead Sciences, and in 2008, he was appointed Chairman of the Board of Directors (Li & De Clercq, 2022).

As CEO, he focused on creating innovative drugs to treat viral infections that significantly threaten people's lives. For instance, Gilead Sciences developed Altripla, which became the most prescribed drug for HIV-infected patients in the United States (Yang et al., 2022). The company also conducts research to develop treatments for oncology, pulmonology, and viral hepatitis. In December 2013, Sovaldi, a drug for treating chronic hepatitis C, was approved and launched on the market, and by the end of 2014, around 117,000 patients had received the necessary therapy. Gilead Sciences' success was significant: revenue and net profit growth from 2013 to 2014 alone was approximately 150% (Meek, 2014).

As the leader of Gilead Sciences, John Martin greatly emphasised innovation, high product quality, and a spirit of entrepreneurship. He built his team based on the company's core values, ensuring new candidates aligned with the corporate culture. He understood the importance of collaborative effort in achieving goals and focused on developing new leaders to ensure the company's continued success (Garabedian, 2021).

After stepping down as CEO in 2016, Martin remained with Gilead as Executive Chairman until 2018. He passed away on 30 March 2021. It is worth noting that during John C. Martin's 20-year tenure as CEO, Gilead Sciences' market capitalisation increased tenfold, reaching $120 billion, and 20 innovative drugs were brought to market. Many of these drugs, particularly those for treating HIV, hepatitis B, and hepatitis C, were truly revolutionary and saved lives in many countries around the world (Lou et al., 2022).

## Appendix C: Biography of Charles R. 'Cork' Walgreen

Charles R. 'Cork' Walgreen, the grandson of Walgreens' founder Charles Walgreen, was born in 1935. In 1958, he graduated from the University of Michigan with a degree in pharmacy. He immediately began working for Walgreens as a pharmacist and regional manager. He soon joined the board of directors and, in 1971, at the age of 33, became the company's CEO. At that time, Walgreens owned 546 pharmacies across various states, a restaurant business, and stores. The company's market capitalisation was $164 million (Collins, 2001; WBA, 2016).

With the arrival of a new leader, strategic changes began in the company as Charles Walgreen set a goal to transform an ordinary family business into a leader in the US pharmacy market. To achieve this, a decision was made to sell the restaurant business – about 500 restaurants – within five years. Dan Jornd, Charles Cork Walgreen's successor as head of Walgreens, emphasised that this decision was resolute. When, six months after the decision was made, someone remarked that there was still time – five years – Charles Walgreen III responded, 'You have four and a half years left; I said "five years" six months ago, so now there are only four and a half left' (Collins, 2001, p. 32). The format of the pharmacies was also changed, and a programme for their effective management was introduced, focusing on profitability per customer visit. Various innovations were implemented as part of Walgreens' new vision for development: to become the most convenient pharmacy with high profitability per customer visit.

By 1975, the work of Charles R. 'Cork' Walgreen and his team had already increased the company's market capitalisation to $1 billion. In 1981, Walgreens became one of the first companies to use the Intercom electronic system to connect all its pharmacies into a single information network. In the early 1990s, Walgreens introduced drive-thru pharmacies, similar to McDonald's restaurants, and enhanced the Intercom system. Charles Walgreen stepped down as CEO in 1998 after 23 years of leading Walgreens. During his tenure, the company's market capitalisation grew exponentially from $164 million to a staggering $16 billion, and its stock price outpaced those of companies such as General Electric, Merck, Coca-Cola, and Intel (Collins, 2001).

Walgreens currently operates nearly 9,000 locations across 53 states and territories in the United States. In 2014, Walgreens entered the international market under the WBA brand after merging with the European pharmacy chain Alliance Boots Holdings. WBA now operates nearly 4,000 retail stores worldwide, including in the UK, Thailand, the Republic of Ireland, Mexico, and Chile. They also own a German pharmaceutical wholesale company (WBA, n.d.). In 2023, the American Business Awards recognised Walgreens Boots Alliance as the Most Innovative Company of the Year (Russo, 2023).

## Appendix D: Albert Bourla and the history of the creation of a COVID-19 vaccine

Albert Bourla was born in Thessaloniki, Greece, on 21 October 1961. He graduated from the Aristotle University of Thessaloniki, earning a Doctor of Veterinary Medicine degree in 1985. He also holds a PhD in the Biotechnology of Reproduction from the same institution. Bourla joined Pfizer in 1993, beginning his career in the Animal Health Division in Greece. Over the years, he held various leadership positions within the company, including Technical Director of the Pfizer Animal Health Division in Greece (1993–2001); Director, Vice President, and Area President of the Pfizer Animal Health Division

(2001–2010); General Manager at Pfizer (2010–2014); Group President at Pfizer (2014–2016); Group President of Pfizer Innovative Health (2016–2018); and COO of Pfizer (2018–2019) (National Journal, n.d.).

Bourla, who took the helm as CEO of Pfizer in January 2019, just a year before the COVID-19 pandemic struck, faced an ambitious challenge: to develop an effective vaccine within months against a viral disease that had claimed the lives of millions worldwide. Bourla's leadership was instrumental in rallying his team and instilling the enthusiasm and confidence needed to tackle the project. As he later remarked, 'We had nothing but problems' (Whipple, 2022). The COVID-19 pandemic posed a significant challenge for many pharmaceutical companies globally, necessitating them to achieve extraordinary results – developing an effective vaccine in the shortest possible time and organising its production and logistics on a global scale.

Pfizer was the first to achieve remarkable success when, nine months after beginning the vaccine development process, its vaccine's efficacy was confirmed at 95%. This allowed the FDA, which had set a minimum efficacy bar at 50%, to authorise the vaccine immediately (Fleischmann, 2022). Albert Bourla noted, 'It became obvious at a certain point that we were the drivers of the largest hope for the most important thing in the world at that time' (Whipple, 2022). This incredible success was made possible by the leadership of Albert Bourla and his team. The SWAT team comprised 11 Pfizer's most senior employees responsible for the scientific research, testing, production, delivery, and analysis of the vaccine's effectiveness.

One of Pfizer's key challenges was using a new and untested technology – the mRNA molecule. This technology, being studied by scientists from the German biopharmaceutical company BioNTech, was a risky but innovative choice. Bourla, following his team's recommendations, invested in creating a COVID-19 vaccine based on mRNA technology. This bold move, backed by the team's extensive expertise, significantly influenced Pfizer's success. At the same time, the team needed to build the production capacity to manufacture hundreds of millions of vaccine doses and carefully plan and execute the logistics for distributing them to numerous countries. These processes were carried out under significant time pressure, leading to emergencies and various challenges. Despite this, the team's adaptability and determination under Bourla's leadership enabled them to succeed. The vaccine was made available to millions worldwide within a year of the pandemic's onset (Fleischmann, 2022).

As a result, Pfizer achieved record sales in 2021 and significantly strengthened its leadership position in the pharmaceutical market. Pfizer's success stemmed partly from its organisational values: courage, excellence, equity, and joy. According to Dr Bourla, thinking big, maintaining high standards, treating all stakeholders fairly – including patients in disadvantaged countries – and taking pride in their work were key to the company's role in combating COVID-19 (Bourla, 2021).

## Appendix E: Biography of Daniel Vasella

Daniel Vasella was born in 1953 in Fribourg, Switzerland. He obtained his medical degree from the University of Bern. Later, in 1989, he completed the management programme at Harvard Business School, and in 2002, he was awarded a doctorate from the University of Basel. In 1984, after completing his studies, he began working as a doctor at the University Hospital in Bern. In 1987, Daniel Vasella joined the pharmaceutical company Sandoz Pharma as an intern and later worked in its American representative office. His exceptional organisational talents and leadership abilities became evident when he served as a product manager, promoting the antitumour drug Sandostatin to market. Vasella successfully coordinated the efforts of teams involved in development, clinical research, production, and marketing, resulting in the drug's successful launch and widespread use in managing the side effects of certain types of cancer. By 2001, Sandostatin's sales had reached nearly $500 million. Notably, the standard practice at the time often involved disjointed and isolated activities among departments responsible for research, production, and marketing, which frequently led to challenges such as the economic infeasibility of production (Encyclopedia.com, n.d.).

In 1993, Vasella returned to Switzerland, initially serving as COO, and in 1995, he assumed the position of CEO of Sandoz. In 1996, he initiated one of the largest mergers in the pharmaceutical industry, uniting the two giants Sandoz and Ciba-Geigy to create Novartis. This merger allowed the companies to combine resources and consolidate their capabilities. The business model was built on a diversification strategy, with an emphasis not only on the creation of original drugs but also on other healthcare products. Despite this diversification, R&D remained a priority for Novartis, accounting for up to 19% of the company's total annual income (Notable Biographies, n.d.).

In 2001, Vasella's efforts paid off in full when the revolutionary drug Gleevec, used to treat chronic myeloid leukaemia, was launched. As the drug's creator, Dr Druker, remarked: 'For a lot of people, Gleevec was simply too good to be true. But these once-dying patients were getting out of bed, dancing, going hiking, doing yoga. The drug was amazing' (National Cancer Institute, 2018). By 2003, Novartis's sales in the United States had grown by 19%, making it the fastest-growing company in the industry (Armstrong, 2009).

Later, Vasella initiated further expansion into the global market, acquiring pharmaceutical companies in the United States and Canada and the largest producer of generic drugs, the German pharmaceutical company Hexal. In the early 2000s, Vasella was one of the first business leaders to reorient the company towards creating biological drugs, making a significant leap from chemistry to molecular biology and engineering. The Novartis Institute for Biomedical Research was established in Cambridge, Massachusetts, and Dr Mark Fishman, a leading scientist in the field of biomedical research, was appointed as the head of this division (Armstrong, 2009).

Daniel Vasella described his leadership model as 'Top Down, Bottom Up, Top Down', emphasising communicating the company's vision and strategy, developing the compensation system, and gathering employee ideas to help drive the company's growth. In addition, Vasella sought to introduce a more aggressive, American management style to the European company, which he believed was most suitable for a harsh competitive environment (Encyclopedia.com, n.d.).

Daniel Vasella received widespread international recognition. In 2004, Time magazine named him one of the 100 most influential people in the world, and readers of the Financial Times voted him the most influential business leader in Europe over the past 25 years. In 2010, he stepped down as CEO of the company, and in 2013, he resigned as Chairman of the Board of Directors (Notable Biographies, n.d.). Peter Young, president of Young & Partners, remarked on Vasella's tenure as CEO of Novartis: 'managing the volatilities of a diversified healthcare company successfully for more than a decade is very rare' (Armstrong, 2009).

## Appendix F: Roy Vagelos and Mectizan Donation Program

In the 1980s, scientists at Merck synthesised an API, ivermectin, capable of combating river blindness (onchocerciasis). This disease affected populations in Africa and Central and South America. At that time, around 85 million people in 35 countries across Africa, Central Asia, and Latin America were at risk. Approximately 300,000 people had lost their sight due to onchocerciasis, about 1 million suffered from various vision problems, and 18 million were infected. Over several years, millions of dollars were required to research, test, produce, and distribute ivermectin. However, the target market segment for this drug consisted of residents of small communities in impoverished countries. Roy Vagelos, head of R&D at Merck, decided to lead the project. He was confident that he would find sponsors within the government to help provide people suffering from onchocerciasis with the drug Mectizan (the trade name for the brand whose API is ivermectin). Vagelos believed this would help reimburse the costs associated with the research and production of the drug. However, these efforts were ultimately unsuccessful. The US government and the WHO refused to provide assistance. Vagelos, by then the CEO and Chairman of the Board of Directors at the pharmaceutical company Merck, decided to take on the financial responsibility for distributing Mectizan to remote areas in impoverished countries. A committee of leading world scientists was also established to develop programmes to provide pharmaceutical care to patients with river blindness in the world's most remote regions.

Since 1987, 2.9 million doses have been produced, with various sponsors and organisations, including the World Bank, WHO, and the Carter Center, joining the project. However, the financial responsibility for the production and distribution of Mectizan remained primarily with Merck (Vagelos & Galambos, 2006).

The MDP is one of the longest-running initiatives providing patients with pharmaceutical care to treat a specific disease – onchocerciasis. Thanks to MDP, more than 4.4 billion doses of medication have been donated to 49 countries, with the programme reaching over 300 million people annually (Merck, 2022). In many respects, due to MDP, Merck has gained wide recognition as a socially responsible corporation; for instance, in 1988, Fortune magazine named Merck as America's most admired company (Friedland, 1989). The programme has garnered full support from internal stakeholders, including shareholders and employees, who take pride in being part of a company with a positive corporate reputation.

## Appendix G: Biography of Filya Zhebrovska

Filya Zhebrovska was born on 24 March 1950 in Nemyrintsi, Zhytomyr Oblast, Ukraine. She graduated from the Kyiv Institute of National Economy, earning her degree in economics. In 1998, she attained the academic title of Candidate of Economic Sciences. Zhebrovska began her career in the pharmaceutical industry in 1980 as the Chief Accountant of the Kyiv Chemical-Pharmaceutical Plant, later renamed JSC 'Farmak'. Her financial expertise and strategic thinking led to her rapid promotion to Deputy Director for Economics and Finance in 1990, followed by Financial Director in 1991. By 1995, Zhebrovska was appointed Chairperson of the Board and General Director when Farmak was in a dire situation. The company faced severe financial struggles, outdated equipment, and a lack of competitive positioning. Zhebrovska spearheaded a transformative modernisation, transitioning Farmak from a producer of APIs to a manufacturer of high-quality finished pharmaceutical products (Politeka, n.d.).

Under her leadership, Farmak became the leading pharmaceutical company in Ukraine, with exports to over 60 countries, including 15 in the European Union. The company reinvests up to 90% of its profits annually into research and development, resulting in the launch of around 20 new pharmaceutical products each year (Farmak, no data). In 2017, after more than two decades as General Director, Zhebrovska transitioned to the role of Chairperson of the Board of Directors, ensuring Farmak's ongoing strategic growth and resilience (Politeka, n.d.).

Zhebrovska has been instrumental in aligning Farmak with European pharmaceutical standards and promoting Ukraine's integration into the global pharmaceutical market. In 2015, Farmak acquired the Polish company Nordfarm, and since 2023, it has actively pursued expansion into the European market by acquiring assets in Poland, the Czech Republic, and Slovakia. In 2024, Farmak acquired the British A&S Group of companies, and in 2025, it plans to launch a newly built manufacturing facility in Barcelona, Spain. All international assets have been consolidated under the Farmak International brand (Farmak, 2024a). Filya Zhebrovska's motto as the leader of Ukraine's leading pharmaceutical company is 'Medicine Without Borders', reflecting her belief that medicines and their quality are matters of health and, at times, life itself (PB News, 2024).

Despite the numerous political and economic challenges Farmak faces, Filya Zhebrovska has consistently demonstrated exceptional leadership traits. She has remarked that persistence in achieving goals and the ability to move forward despite difficulties are essential attributes of effective leadership. Moreover, Zhebrovska has continuously emphasised the importance of building trust within a team and the ability to unite skilled and motivated people around a shared vision (Forbes, 2023).

Beyond her professional achievements, Zhebrovska's contributions extend to social impact. The Zhebrovska Family Charitable Foundation funds education, healthcare, and cultural initiatives, advancing medical infrastructure and preserving Ukrainian heritage. The foundation also played a critical role in supporting communities and healthcare services during the war in Ukraine (Marie Claire, 2023).

Filya Zhebrovska is the author of 120 scientific publications, including a monograph, and holds 100 patents in Ukraine. Zhebrovska's leadership and innovations have earned her numerous accolades. She holds the Order of Merit in all three classes (I–III) (Politeka, n.d.). In 2022, she was included in Forbes' '50 Over 50' global list, celebrating influential women driving innovation and impact beyond the age of 50 (Marie Claire, 2023). In 2024, NV magazine recognised her as one of the 'People of the Decade' for her contributions to Ukraine's pharmaceutical industry (Farmak, 2024b).

## Appendix H: Malvinder Mohan Singh and Ranbaxy Laboratories

Ranbaxy Laboratories, an Indian pharmaceutical company, was founded in 1961 and managed for many years by the Singh family. It became one of India's largest pharmaceutical companies, producing hundreds of generic drugs and supplying them to many countries worldwide.

In 2005, Malvinder Mohan Singh became the company's leader with a vision to create a sustainable, profitable business in the US market, aiming for a turnover of $1 billion by 2015. This goal was prioritised for all employees, often at the expense of developing high-quality, effective, and safe medicines. The neglect of ethical principles in the creation, research, and production of drugs led to the construction of large-scale falsification and fraud schemes within the company. Ranbaxy falsified reports on drug testing results for stability, solubility, impurity analysis, the presence of APIs, and more. The company had established a scheme for the large-scale purchase of original drugs abroad and their delivery to Ranbaxy factories to falsify test results, including bioequivalence tests. The data submitted by the Indian company Ranbaxy to the FDA in the United States was falsified by approximately 50–60%, a figure also applicable to Western European countries. For India and developing regions such as Africa, the Middle East, Southeast Asia, South America, Eastern Europe, and Central Asia, the data was falsified by 100%. Later, the manager of Ranbaxy's analytical research department attempted to justify this by claiming that the systematic data recording during research is not typical of Indian culture. Ranbaxy intimidated individuals and even threatened those who interfered with their deception and falsification with direct physical violence. In 2010, the FDA initiated a comprehensive review of Ranbaxy under its strictest procedure, the Application Integrity Policy, which required the re-registration of all the company's drugs. By then, tens of thousands of complaints from patients and doctors regarding low-quality generics had already been recorded. In 2012, the FDA fined Ranbaxy $500 million. By 2014, the company had effectively ceased to exist, having been absorbed by Sun Pharma following a series of scandals and lawsuits (Eban, 2019).

It is worth noting that Ranbaxy was far from the only company that committed such serious violations. Eban (2019) concluded that there are systemic and deliberate standards violations in the research, testing, and production of generic drugs. Such violations are not limited to Indian or Chinese companies; all pharmaceutical companies that seek to maximise profits through deception and fraud pose a risk to the health and lives of patients.

## Appendix I: Biography of Kiran Mazumdar-Shaw

Kiran Mazumdar-Shaw, the founder and head of the Indian biopharmaceutical company Biocon, was born on 23 March 1953 in Bangalore, India. The daughter of a brewmaster, she initially planned to follow in her father's footsteps. In 1973, she earned a bachelor's degree with honours in zoology from Bangalore University and later obtained a master's degree in brewing from the University of Melbourne. Upon returning to India, Kiran began her career as a brewing intern and worked as a consultant. However, within four years, she met the owner of the Irish company Biocon Biochemicals, who became her partner in founding Biocon India in 1978, a company focused on enzyme production (Hollar, 2024).

In its early stages, Biocon faced significant challenges. Many banks were reluctant to provide loans as biotechnology was a relatively new field in India. Furthermore, there was widespread bias and scepticism regarding her gender and age. Hiring employees also proved difficult, as many hesitated to work under a woman's leadership. Despite these initial obstacles, Kiran Mazumdar-Shaw persevered, and within a year, Biocon began exporting its products to the United States and Europe. Over time, the company shifted its focus to the pharmaceutical market, reinvesting profits into research and development. In 2001, Biocon became the first Indian company to receive approval from the US FDA to produce lovastatin. By 2003, the company's profits had increased by more than 40%, enabling the development of next-generation bio-insulin, Insugen. Following Biocon's highly successful initial public offering (IPO) in 2004, the company's valuation soared, making Kiran Mazumdar-Shaw the wealthiest woman in India (Hollar, 2024).

Today, Biocon is recognised as a dynamic and innovative global biopharmaceutical company, with products distributed in over 120 countries, including North America, Europe, Japan, Australia, and emerging markets (Biocon, 2024). In 2024, Biocon reported annual revenues exceeding $1.7 billion (PitchBook, n.d.). The company's business operations are diversified into three key segments: generics, research services, and biosimilars. Biocon produces various APIs and generic drugs in diabetology, oncology, cardiology, and immunotherapy. Through its subsidiary Syngene International Limited, the company provides integrated research, development, and manufacturing services for the pharmaceutical, biotechnology, and agrochemical industries. The biosimilar segment is the largest revenue driver, accounting for approximately 60% of the company's income. It produces insulin and monoclonal antibody biosimilars for treating various diseases (Biocon, 2024). This segment has seen significant growth; in 2022, Biocon Biologics acquired the biosimilars business of the US pharmaceutical company Viatris for $3.3 billion (Forbes, n.d.).

Kiran Mazumdar-Shaw views her business activities through the lens of service to society. For her, innovation and commerce are powerful tools for social progress, focusing on accessibility and long-term impact. She stated, 'My legacy is going to be in affordable healthcare. I am willing to invest in developing that model and the policies around it' (Forbes, n.d.). Beyond her business achievements, she invests significantly in healthcare and education, particularly in India's poorest regions. She has contributed to the development of medical infrastructure and the establishment of clinics. For instance, she played a pivotal role in founding a cancer centre in Bangalore that treats people regardless of income or social status (Forbes, n.d.).

Ranked among the top 100 most influential women globally, Kiran Mazumdar-Shaw secured the 76th spot in Forbes' 2023 list (Forbes, n.d.). She has received numerous awards, including a gold medal for her contributions to science in 2014. In 2020, she was named the EY World Entrepreneur of the Year and recognised as one of the top 20 global biopharmaceutical leaders on The Medicine Maker's Power List (Biocon, n.d.).

## References

Armstrong, W., (2009). The Book on Daniel. *Pharmaceutical Executive* [online], 1 October 2009. Available from: https://www.pharmexec.com/view/book-daniel [Accessed 22 February 2024].

Biocon, (2024). *Who we are* [online], Biocon. Available from: https://www.biocon.com/about-us/who-we-are/ [Accessed 10 December 2024].

Biocon, (n.d.). *Kiran Mazumdar-Shaw: Awards and Recognition* [online], Biocon. Available from: https://www.biocon.com/docs/Kiran-Mazumdar-Shaw-Awards-and-Recognition.pdf [Accessed 26 December 2024].

Bourla, A., (2021). The CEO of Pfizer on developing a vaccine in record time. *Harvard Business Review* [online], May. Available from: https://hbr.org/2021/05/the-ceo-of-pfizer-on-developing-a-vaccine-in-record-time [Accessed 07 February 2024].

Collins, J., (2001). *Good to Great*. London: Random House Business Books.

Eban, K., (2019). *Bottle of Lies: The Inside Story of the Generic Drug Boom*. New York: Ecco Press.

Encyclopedia.com, (n.d.). *Vasella, Daniel 1953 – International Directory of Business Biographies*. Encyclopedia.com [online]. Available from: https://www.encyclopedia.com/economics/news-wires-white-papers-and-books/vasella-daniel-1953 [Accessed 15 January 2024].

Farmak, (2024a). *Medicines for the world: 'Farmak' began expansion into five European countries, investing tens of millions of euros. What is it aiming for?* [online]. Farmak. Available from: https://farmak.ua/publication/liki-dlya-svitu-farmak-pochav-ekspansiyu-u-pyat-evropejskih-krayin-investuvavshi-desyatki-miljoniv-evro-na-shho-vin-rozrahovue/ [Accessed 18 December 2024] [Ukrainian].

Farmak, (2024b). *Filya Zhebrovska became the person of the decade according to NV* [online]. Farmak. Available from: https://farmak.ua/en/news/filya-zhebrovska-became-the-person-of-the-decade-according-to-nv/ [Accessed 17 December 2024].

Farmak, (n.d.). *About us* [online]. *Farmak*. Available from: https://farmak.ua/en/about/ [Accessed 17 December 2024].

Fleischmann, A., (2022). Albert Bourla. Chairman and CEO, Pfizer. *Leadership Matters* [online], 5 April 2022. Available from: https://www.leadershipmattersshow.com/episodes/albert-bourla [Accessed 15 February 2024].

Forbes, (2023). *Filia Zhebrovska: 'A strong, cohesive team is the main asset of any business'* [online]. Forbes Ukraine. Available from: https://forbes.ua/company/filya-zhebrovska-silna-zgurtovana-komanda-golovniy-aktiv-bud-yakogo-biznesu-28062023-14430 [Accessed 15 December 2024] [Ukrainian].

Forbes, (n.d.). *Kiran Mazumdar-Shaw* [online], Forbes. Available from: https://www.forbes.com/profile/kiran-mazumdar-shaw/?list=power-women [Accessed 26 December 2024].

Friedland, S., (1989). *Pharmaceutical company shares its harvest of achievement. The New York Times* [online], 5 March 1989. Available from: https://www.nytimes.com/1989/03/05/nyregion/pharmaceutical-company-shares-its-harvest-of-achievement.html [Accessed 05 April 2024].

Garabedian, C., (2021). The Glory of John Martin: An Understated Leader Who Built a Biotech Powerhouse. *Timmerman Report* [online], 5 April 2021. Available from: https://timmermanreport.com/2021/04/the-glory-of-john-martin-an-understated-leader-who-built-a-biotech-powerhouse/ [Accessed 15 December 2023].

Gurowitz, M., (2015). The legacy of Dr. Paul Janssen: How a "funny idea" helped change the course of modern medicine. *Johnson & Johnson* [online], 11 September 2015. Available from: https://www.jnj.com/the-legacy-of-dr-paul-janssen-how-a-funny-idea-helped-change-the-course-of-modern-medicine [Accessed 11 December 2023].

Hollar, S., (2024), Mazumdar-Shaw. *Encyclopedia Britannica* [online]. 4 December 2024. Available from: https://www.britannica.com/money/Kiran-Mazumdar-Shaw [Accessed 22 December 2024].

Johnson & Johnson, (n.d.). *Dr Paul Janssen Award* [online]. Johnson & Johnson. Available from: https://www.pauljanssenaward.com/ [Accessed 07 March 2024].

Lewi, P.J., & Smith, A., (2007). Successful pharmaceutical discovery: Paul Janssen's concept of drug research. *R&D Management*, 37(4), 355–362. https://doi.org/10.1111/j.1467-9310.2007.00481.x

Li, G., & De Clercq, E. (2022). A medicinal chemist who reshaped the antiviral drug industry: John Charles Martin (1951-2021). *Medicinal Research Reviews*, 42(2), 647–653. https://doi.org/10.1002/med.21858

Lou, L.L., Flood, A., Yang, T., & Whitley, R.J., (2022). Commentary: John C. Martin (1951–2021). *Antiviral Therapy*, 27(2). https://journals.sagepub.com/doi/full/10.1177/13596535211067895

Marie Claire, (2023). *Instead of tears – help for the Armed Forces: Unbreakable Ukrainian women as a separate front* [online]. Marie Claire. Available from: https://marieclaire.ua/fashion/zamist-sliz-dopomoga-zsu-nezlamni-ukrayinki-yak-okremij-front/ [Accessed 18 December 2024] [Ukrainian].

Meek, T., (2014). 117,000 hepatitis C patients receive Sovaldi so far. *PMLive* [online], 29 October 2014. Available from: https://pmlive.com/pharma_news/117000_hepatitis_c_patients_receive_sovaldi_so_far_610646 [Accessed 3 January 2025].

Merck, (2022). *Mectizan: Pioneering a community-directed approach* [online]. Merck. Available from: https://www.merck.com/stories/mectizan/#:~:text=Pioneering%20a%20community%2Ddirected%20approach&text=The%20program%20reaches%20more%20than,where%20Mectizan%20has%20been%20distributed [Accessed 04 April 2024].

National Cancer Institute, (2018). *Gleevec: A targeted cancer treatment* [online]. National Cancer Institute. Available from: https://www.cancer.gov/research/progress/discovery/gleevec [Accessed 03 February 2024].

National Journal, (n.d.). *Business leaders: Albert Bourla* [online]. National Journal. Available from: https://go.nationaljournal.com/rs/556-YEE-969/images/Business-Leaders_Albert_Bourla.pdf [Accessed 10 August 2024].

Notable Biographies, (n.d.). *Daniel Vasella* [online]. Notable Biographies. Available from: https://www.notablebiographies.com/newsmakers2/2005-Pu-Z/Vasella-Daniel.html [Accessed 20 January 2024].

PB News, (2024). *Forbes interviewed the chair of the supervisory board of 'Farmak', Filya Zhebrovska* [online]. PB News. Available from: https://pb-news.info/2024/07/11/forbes-vzyav-intervyu-u-golovy-naglyadovoyi-rady-farmak-fili-zhebrovskoyi/ [Accessed 15 December 2024] [Ukrainian].

PitchBook, (n.d.). *Biocon: Company overview* [online], PitchBook. Available from: https://pitchbook.com/profiles/company/53660-35#overview [Accessed 22 December 2024].

Politeka, (n.d.). *Filia Ivanivna Zhebrovska: The dossier of the pharmaceutical queen who revived a chemical-pharmaceutical plant and made it an industry leader* [online]. Politeka. Available from: https://politeka.net/uk/person/1107597-zhebrovskaja-filja-ivanovna-dose-farmacevticheskoj-korolevy-kotoraja-vozrodila-himiko-farmacevticheskij-zavod-i-vyvela-v-lidery-otrasli#i-4 [Accessed 17 December 2024] [Ukrainian].

Russo, E., (2023). WBA wins Gold Stevie Award for Most Innovative Company of the Year. *WBA* [online], 28 April 2023. Available from: https://www.walgreensbootsalliance.com/news-media/our-stories/wba-wins-gold-stevie-award-most-innovative-company-year [Accessed 30 January 2024].

Vagelos, P.R., & Galambos, L., (2006). *The Moral Corporation – Merck Experiences*. New York, NY: Cambridge University Press.

WBA, (2016). *Charles R. Walgreen III, former Walgreen Co. Chairman and CEO, dies at age 80*. WBA [online]. Available from: https://www.walgreensbootsalliance.com/news-media/press-releases/2016/charles-r-walgreen-iii-former-walgreen-co-chairman-and-ceo-dies-at-age-80 [Accessed 30 January 2024].

WBA, (n.d.). *About us* [online]. WBA. Available from: https://www.walgreensbootsalliance.com/about-us [Accessed 30 January 2024].

Whipple, T., (2022). Billions at stake, endless waiting, an angry Trump: the Pfizer's CEO great vax hunt. *The Sydney Morning Herald* [online], 09 April 2022. Available from: https://www.smh.com.au/national/billions-at-stake-endless-waiting-an-angry-trump-the-pfizer-ceo-s-great-vax-hunt-20220304-p5a1q7.html [Accessed 25 February 2024].

Yang, T., Oliyai, R., & Kent, K.M., (2022). The making of the one pill – Developing single tablet regimens for HIV and for HCV. *Antiviral Therapy*, 27(2). https://journals.sagepub.com/doi/10.1177/13596535211067606?icid=int.sj-abstract.similar-articles.2

# Index

Note: **Bold** indicates tables and *italics* indicates figures in the text.

For Product Safety Concerns and Information please contact our EU representative GPSR@taylorandfrancis.com Taylor & Francis Verlag GmbH, Kaufingerstraße 24, 80331 München, Germany

Printed and bound by CPI Group (UK) Ltd, Croydon, CR0 4YY
14/09/2026
02216223-0010